THE EVOLUTION OF TECHNOLOGY

TECHNOLOGY 4.0

MR. NIKHIL KUMAR

Copyright © Mr. NIKHIL KUMAR
All Rights Reserved.

This book has been self-published with all reasonable efforts taken to make the material error-free by the author. No part of this book shall be used, reproduced in any manner whatsoever without written permission from the author, except in the case of brief quotations embodied in critical articles and reviews.

The Author of this book is solely responsible and liable for its content including but not limited to the views, representations, descriptions, statements, information, opinions and references ["Content"]. The Content of this book shall not constitute or be construed or deemed to reflect the opinion or expression of the Publisher or Editor. Neither the Publisher nor Editor endorse or approve the Content of this book or guarantee the reliability, accuracy or completeness of the Content published herein and do not make any representations or warranties of any kind, express or implied, including but not limited to the implied warranties of merchantability, fitness for a particular purpose. The Publisher and Editor shall not be liable whatsoever for any errors, omissions, whether such errors or omissions result from negligence, accident, or any other cause or claims for loss or damages of any kind, including without limitation, indirect or consequential loss or damage arising out of use, inability to use, or about the reliability, accuracy or sufficiency of the information contained in this book.

Made with ♥ on the Notion Press Platform
www.notionpress.com

To the curious minds, the tireless explorers, and the visionaries who dared to dream beyond the confines of the present:

In this digital odyssey, we traverse the epochs—from the flickering glow of vacuum tubes to the pulsing currents of quantum circuits. We honor those who forged the path, their hands stained with ink and solder, their hearts ablaze with possibility.

To the pioneers of yesteryears, who whispered secrets to punch cards and danced with mainframes under moonlit skies:

Your legacy pulses through silicon veins, woven into the fabric of our existence. You birthed the binary cosmos—the realm where electrons pirouette, algorithms sing, and data whispers its truths.

And to the architects of Technology 4.0, the weavers of neural networks and quantum entanglements:

You stand at the precipice, gazing into the singularity. Your code is incantation; your algorithms, spells. With each line, you summon intelligence from the ether, birthing sentience in circuits.

This book is for you—the dreamers, the coders, the cyborgs, and the stargazers.

May your bytes be ever efficient, your interfaces seamless, and your disruptions benevolent.

With boundless curiosity,

Mr. Nikhil Kumar

Contents

Foreword

As we stand at the threshold of a new era in human history, it is fitting that we take a moment to reflect on the journey that has brought us here. The evolution of technology has been a defining feature of our species, shaping our lives, our cultures, and our understanding of the world around us.

This book is a masterful telling of that story, weaving together the threads of innovation and experimentation that have transformed human civilization. From the earliest sparks of ingenuity to the latest breakthroughs in artificial intelligence, the author takes us on a sweeping narrative that illuminates the triumphs and setbacks, the visionaries and inventors, and the social and cultural contexts that have shaped the development of technology.

What emerges from these pages is a rich tapestry of human creativity and perseverance, as well as a sobering reminder of the challenges and uncertainties that lie ahead. As we hurtle towards a future of unprecedented technological advancement, it is more important than ever that we understand the path that has brought us here, and consider the implications of our choices.

This book is a clarion call to anyone interested in the future of humanity, a future that will be shaped by the technologies we create and the choices we make. It is a testament to the power of human ingenuity and a reminder of our responsibility to use that power wisely.

I am honored to commend this book to you, and I have no doubt that it will inspire, educate, and provoke readers to think deeply about the evolution of technology and its impact on our world."
Mr. Nikhil Kumar

Date: - 20/09/2024

Preface

The evolution of technology has been a long and winding road, marked by twists and turns that have transformed human civilization in profound ways. From the earliest stone tools to the latest artificial intelligence systems, technology has been the driving force behind human progress, shaping our lives, our cultures, and our understanding of the world around us.

This book tells the story of that journey, tracing the development of technology from its humble beginnings to the present day. It is a story of innovation and experimentation, of triumph and disaster, of visionaries and inventors who have pushed the boundaries of what is possible.

Through this narrative, I aim to provide a comprehensive and accessible history of technology, highlighting the key milestones, discoveries, and innovations that have shaped our world. I explore the social, cultural, and economic contexts in which technologies emerged, and examine the impact they have had on human society.

This book is not just a chronicle of technological progress, but also a reflection on the human experience. It is a story of how technology has changed us, and how we have changed technology. It is a story of hope and fear, of promise and peril, of the boundless potential of human ingenuity and the uncertain consequences of our actions.

I hope that this book will inspire readers to think critically about the role of technology in their lives, and to consider the possibilities and challenges that lie ahead. Join me on this journey through the evolution of technology, and discover how it has shaped our world and will continue to shape our future."

Author Name: - Mr. Nikhil Kumar
Date: -20/09/2024

Acknowledgements

"I would like to express my deepest gratitude to the individuals and organizations who have supported me throughout the journey of writing this book.

First and foremost, I thank my family, Specialy my father who have endured countless hours of my absence and distraction, yet remained unwavering in their encouragement and love. To my colleagues and peers in the field of technology, I appreciate your insights, critiques, and generosity in sharing your expertise. Your contributions have enriched this book and expanded my understanding of new Technology. I am also indebted to the researchers, innovators, and thought leaders who have pioneered the concepts and advancements explored in this book. Your groundbreaking work has paved the way for this revolution, and I hope this book does justice to your achievements.

To my editor and publisher, I thank you for your guidance, patience, and dedication in shaping this manuscript into its final form. Your expertise has been invaluable. Additionally, I acknowledge the support of Ies Instituteof technology Bopal who have provided access to resources, data, and networks that have informed my research.

Lastly, I thank the readers who will engage with this book, and I hope that it will inspire, educate, and empower you to navigate the exciting landscape of Technology. This book is a testament to the power of collaboration, innovation, and human curiosity. I am humbled to be a part of this journey and look forward to continuing the conversation about the future of technology.

Prologue

In the beginning, humanity's relationship with technology was simple and utilitarian. The first tools, fashioned from stone and bone, were extensions of our hands, amplifying our ability to hunt, gather, and survive. As millennia passed, our ingenuity transformed these rudimentary implements into sophisticated machines, each leap forward marking a new chapter in the story of human progress.

The Industrial Revolution heralded an era of unprecedented change, where steam engines and mechanized factories reshaped societies and economies. This was Technology 1.0, a time when human muscle was augmented by mechanical power. The 20th century brought Technology 2.0, characterized by the advent of electricity, mass production, and the birth of the digital age. Computers, once room-sized behemoths, became personal companions, and the internet connected the world in ways previously unimaginable.

As we stepped into the 21st century, Technology 3.0 emerged, driven by the convergence of digital, biological, and physical systems. Artificial intelligence, biotechnology, and nanotechnology began to blur the lines between the organic and the synthetic, the virtual and the real. Yet, even as these advancements transformed our lives, they set the stage for an even more profound evolution.

Welcome to Technology 4.0, the dawn of a new era where the boundaries of possibility are continually redefined. This is a world where intelligent systems learn and adapt, where machines not only perform tasks but also make decisions. It is a time of cyber-physical systems, the Internet of Things, and smart cities. Here, data is the new currency, and connectivity is the lifeblood of innovation.

In this book, we will journey through the epochs of technological evolution, exploring the milestones that have brought us to this pivotal moment. We will delve into the transformative power of Technology 4.0, examining its potential to reshape industries, societies, and the very fabric of our existence. As we navigate this brave new world, we will ponder the ethical, philosophical, and practical implications of living in an age where technology is not just a tool, but a partner in our quest for progress.

Join me as we embark on this exploration of the past, present, and future of technology. Together, we will uncover the stories of visionaries and innovators who dared to dream beyond the horizon, and we will contemplate the limitless possibilities that lie ahead in the age of Technology 4.0.

ONE

ARTIFICIAL INTELLIGENCE

1. Artificial General Intelligence (AGI)

Artificial General Intelligence (AGI) refers to a type of artificial intelligence that aims to replicate human cognitive abilities across a wide range of tasks. Unlike narrow AI, which is designed for specific tasks (like language translation or image recognition), AGI would have the ability to understand, learn, and apply knowledge in a manner similar to human intelligence.

AGI is AI with capabilities that rival those of a human. While purely theoretical at this stage, someday AGI may replicate human-like cognitive abilities including reasoning, problem solving, perception, learning, and language comprehension. When AI's abilities are indistinguishable from those of a human, it will have passed what is known as the Turing test, first proposed by 20th-century computer scientist Alan Turing. But let's not get ahead of ourselves. AI has made significant strides in recent years, but no AI tool to date has passed the Turing test. We're still far from reaching a point where AI tools can understand, communicate, and act with the same nuance and sensitivity of a human—and, critically, understand the meaning behind it. Most researchers and academics believe we are decades away from realizing AGI; a few even predict we won't see AGI this century (or ever). Rodney Brooks, a roboticist at the Massachusetts Institute of Technology and cofounder of iRobot, believes AGI won't arrive until the year 2300. If you're thinking that AI already seems pretty smart, that's understandable. We've seen gen AI do remarkable things in recent years, from writing code to composing sonnets in seconds. But there's a critical difference between AI and AGI. Although the latest gen AI technologies, including ChatGPT, DALL-E, and others, have been hogging headlines, they are essentially prediction machines—albeit very good ones. In other words, they can predict, with a high degree of accuracy, the answer to a specific prompt because they've been trained on huge amounts of data. This is impressive, but it's not at a human level of performance in terms of creativity, logical reasoning, sensory perception, and other capabilities. By contrast, AGI tools could feature cognitive and emotional abilities (like empathy) indistinguishable from those of a human. Depending on your definition of AGI, they might even be capable of consciously grasping the meaning behind what they're doing. The timing of AGI's emergence is uncertain. But when it does arrive—and it likely will at some point—it's going to be a very big deal for every aspect of our lives, businesses, and societies. Executives can begin working now to better understand the path to machines achieving human-level intelligence and making the transition to a more automated world.

AGI vs. AI: What's the Difference?

AGI is a subcategory of AI, and the former can be seen as an upgraded version of the latter. Artificial intelligence is often trained on data to perform specific tasks or a range of tasks limited to a single context. Many forms of AI rely on algorithms or pre-programmed rules to guide their actions and learn how to operate in a certain environment. Artificial general intelligence, on the other hand, is able to reason and adapt to new environments and different types of data. So instead of depending on predetermined rules to function, AGI embraces a problem-solving and learning approach — similar to humans. Because of its flexibility, AGI is capable of handling more tasks in different industries and sectors.

Future of Artificial General Intelligence

Although AGI is still a way off, rapid progress in the AI field has brought technology closer to achieving AGI. Some predictions even have computers reaching the level of human intelligence as early as 2029. The realization of AGI would mean AI that could act on abstract thinking, common sense, background knowledge, transfer learning and cause and effect. This would open up the possibilities for numerous industries. AGI could perform surgeries in the medical field and bring about autonomous cars in the automotive industry. More ambitious views of AGI even have the technology helping humans address large-scale problems like climate change. With its far-reaching abilities, AGI could automate tasks that typically involve the kind of abstract thinking that only humans are capable of performing. Complex tasks and workflows would become AI-powered, saving organizations more time and money.

Ethical Considerations of Artificial General Intelligence

The benefits of AGI sound promising, but society needs to approach AGI with caution. While AGI hints at a reality where AI can learn more difficult concepts unique to humans, there's reason to question whether AI can understand human ethics. Even advanced technologies like ChatGPT have demonstrated harmful biases related to race and gender. Current issues occurring before the existence of AGI may hint at larger problems emerging under artificial superintelligence — AI that transcends human intelligence. Without the ability to control AI, humans may have to face technology that reproduces devastating biases and makes decisions that go against human ethical standards. Even if humans do control AGI, there's the question of who gets to control it and what kind of power that gives them. For example, Meta already boasts a vast social media business, and the possibility of achieving AGI potentially puts more power in the hands of CEO Mark Zuckerberg. If Zuckerberg follows in the footsteps of AI competitors and decides not to open-source Meta's models, the ability to build AGI becomes further concentrated in the hands of a few corporations. AGI remains an exciting proposition for many industries, but AI is ultimately a reflection of its creator's intentions. Organizations and industry leaders may want to ensure AGI and other forms of AI are developed for benevolent purposes before embracing the technology.

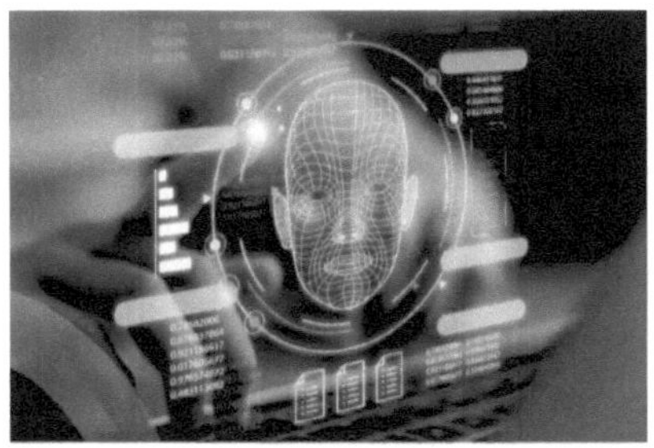

Artificial General Intelligence

2.Deepfake technology

Deepfake technology involves using artificial intelligence (AI) to create realistic but fake audio, video, or images. Deepfake is one of the buzzwords in media technology wherein a person simply takes existing text, picture, video, or audio and then manipulates, i.e., 'fakes' it to look like someone else using advanced artificial intelligence (AI) and neural network (NN) technology. Want to put abusive words in the mouth of your nemesis? Or swap the movie protagonist with your favourite Hollywood superstar? Or do you just want to make yourself dance like Michael Jackson? Then deepfake is what you need! Deepfake content is growing exponentially. Unfortunately, deepfake tech has already been repeatedly used to gain political mileage, to tarnish the image of a rival, or to commit financial fraud.

Deep learning is a type of machine learning based on artificial neural networks, which are inspired by the human brain. The method is used to teach machines how to learn from large amounts of data via multi-layered structures of algorithms. Deepfakes usually employ a deep-learning computer network called a variational auto-encoder, a type of artificial neural network that is normally used for facial recognition. Autoencoders can encode and compress input data, reducing it to a lower dimensional latent space, and then reconstruct it to deliver output data based on the latent representation. In the case of deepfakes, the autoencoders are used to detect facial features, suppressing visual noise and "non-face" elements in the process. The latent representation contains all these basic data that the autoencoder will use to deliver a more versatile model that allows the "face swap", leaning on common features. To make the results more realistic, deepfakes also use Generative Adversarial Networks (GANs). GANs train a "generator" to create new images from the latent representation of the source image, and a "discriminator" to evaluate the realism of the generated materials.

Who invented deepfake technology?

No single person can be credited for inventing deepfake technology as it is based on several previous technologies, such as artificial neural networks (ANNs) and artificial intelligence (AI).

In general, the development of this type of synthetic media can be traced back to the 1990s. But deepfake technology as we know it today often relies on GANs, and GANs didn't exist until 2014 when they were invented by computer scientist Ian Goodfellow.

DEEPFAKE

03.Scientists Want to Use Real Human Brain Cells For AI

Despite AI's impressive triumphs, its computational power pales in comparison with a human brain. Now, scientists unveil a revolutionary path to drive computing forward: organoid intelligence, where human brain cells act as biological hardware. Organoid intelligence (OI) is an emerging field where researchers are developing biological computing using 3D cultures of human brain cells (brain organoids) and brain-machine interface technologies.

These organoids share aspects of brain structure and function that play a key role in cognitive functions like learning and memory. They would essentially serve as biological hardware, and could one day be even more efficient than current computers running AI programs. In a new article published in Frontiers, a large international collaboration led by researchers at John Hopkins University (JHU) details how brain-machine technologies are the newest frontier in biocomputing, and provides a roadmap as to how to make it a reality. The human brain has an incredible capacity to store information: the average noggin can store an estimated 2,500 terabytes, according to the paper. The researchers envision complex 3D cell structures that would be connected to AI and machine learning systems. Researchers have previously combined the biological and synthetic to teach brain cells how to play Pong—a proof of concept that was conducted by some of the same scientists involved in this initiative.

That project involved the creation of a Dish Brain system, where researchers created a brain-computer interface, providing neurons with simple electrical sensory input and feedback that allowed them to "learn" the game. However, the new paper sees even bigger applications than getting cells to play video games. For one, brain organoids could have applications in medicine. The authors write that OI research will allow for the exploration of inter-individual neurodevelopmental and neurodegenerative disorders, and revolutionize drug testing research. Ref: Frontiers; VICE

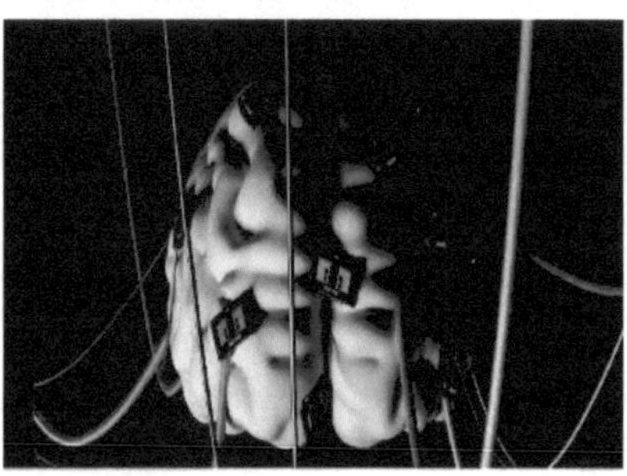

Human Brain Cells

4. Facebook AI's Once Created Their Own Creepy Language

Back in 2017, Facebook release some AI chatbots onto its social network. The result was not at all what they had been expecting the two chatbots began to talk to each other in a strange language that they, but no one else, could understand. When the universe was young, it was more or less uniform, with matter and magnetic fields essentially the same in all directions. But over time, the distribution of dark matter attracted matter to it, forming a gigantic network of dense filaments containing galaxies and clusters, threading between vast voids. This cosmic web was first theoretically proposed in the 1960s, and its structure was modeled in simulations beginning in the 1980s. More recently, astronomers have been able to map it out and observe the glow of its filaments. In the new study, scientists from the Centre for Radio Astronomy Research (ICRAR) have managed to observe radio emissions coming from shockwaves rolling through the cosmic web. Doing so wasn't easy, since the signals are extremely faint and hard to pick out of the background of all the other radio emissions blaring constantly through the universe. So the team instead focused on a variation that's less common – polarized radio signals, which are produced in the cosmic web as the end result of a cascade of processes. Regions of the web that are denser with matter will attract even more matter through gravity. As matter falls into these regions it heats up the gases there, which radiate outwards as shockwaves. When these shockwaves reach the extremely cold voids, that interaction gives off polarized radio light. The team used data from several projects and observatories, including the Global Magneto-Ionic Medium Survey, the Planck Legacy Archive, the Owens Valley Long Wavelength Array, and the Murchison Widefield Array. This allowed them to stack data of detected polarized radio emissions over the top of known cosmic web clusters and filaments, showing that the detections were indeed coming from the web. Ref: journal Science Advances

5.China Says It Will Roll Out Humanoid Robots by 2025

The government is backing burgeoning robotics firms to ensure the ambitious plan comes to fruition. China is hoping to welcome robotkind in just two years' time. The country plans to produce its first humanoid robots by 2025, according to an ambitious blueprint published by the Ministry of Industry and Information (MITT) Technology last week. The MITT says the advanced bipedal droids have the power to reshape the world, carrying out menial, repetitive tasks in farms, factories, and houses to alleviate our workload. "They are expected to become disruptive products after computers, smartphones, and new energy vehicles," the document states. The government will accelerate the development of the robots by funding more young companies in the field, as reported by Bloomberg. Fourier Intelligence is one such Chinese startup hoping to start mass-producing general-purpose humanoid robots by the end of this year. The Fourier GR-1 measures five feet and four inches and weighs around 121 pounds. With 40 joints, the bot reportedly has "unparalleled agility" human-like movement. It can also walk at roughly 3 mph and complete basic tasks. China isn't the only country working on our future robot helpers, of course. In the U.S., Tesla is continuing to refine Optimus. The bipedal humanoid robot has progressed rapidly since the first shaky prototype was revealed at the marque's AI day in 2022. It can now do yoga, in fact. Tesla has yet to announce a firm timetable for when Optimus will hit the market, but CEO Elon Musk has previously said that the $20,000 robot could be ready in three to five years.

Agility Robotics is another U.S. company with "building robots for good." It opened a robot manufacturing facility in Oregon earlier this year that can produce more than 10,000 Digit droids per year. It also recently announced that Amazon will begin testing Digit for use in their operations.

Meanwhile, Boston Dynamics—makers of Spot, the $75,000 robotic dog—has built another decidedly agile bipedal robot. Atlas showed it could move various obstacles earlier this year, after nailing a parkour course in 2021. Boston Dynamic's Atlas is a research platform and not available for purchase, but the robot does show the U.S. is on par with China in terms of droid design.

Humanoid Robots

6.Google's Real Plan with It's Patented Camera-Hat

Google hasn't been very successful when it comes to wearables, but that's not stopping the tech giant. It was granted a patent for a baseball cap with a mounted video camera, used for capturing videos, which you can upload directly to social media. The high-tech cap may be the tech giant's follow-up to its failed Google Glass and could offer competition to similar wearable devices. Hat-and-camera system that offers users an interactive experience for social media purposes, and it can also be used for personal safety. Users could share photos or videos directly from what's been dubbed the Google Hat to a social media account, but the hat's technology could also be useful in an emergency. The patent indicates that the wearable camera hat could protect the user from a threatening situation. The user can activate an emergency situation indicator and cause the wearable camera system to transmit a video feed to an appropriate emergency handling system, potentially deterring a dangerous person near the user. Along with the patent for the Google Hat, the tech company was also granted one for a camera bracelet. Drawings of the bracelet show a digital screen and two camera lenses, but potential application details were not included in the patent application.

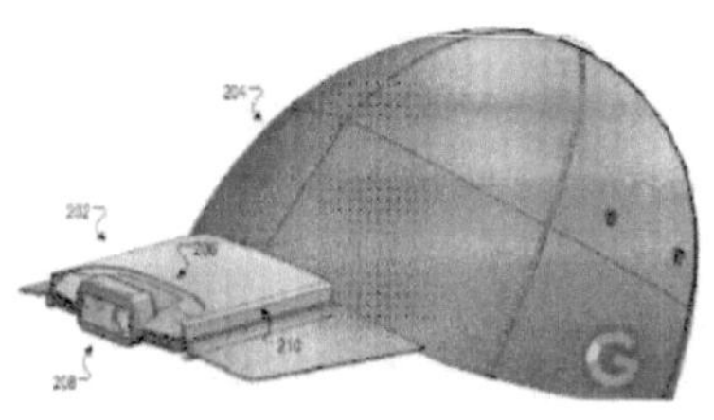

Google Hat

7.Sophia Humanoid Robots

Sophia is a realistic humanoid robot capable of displaying humanlike expressions and interacting with people. It's designed for research, education, and entertainment, and helps promote public discussion about AI ethics and the future of robotics. Sophia was a social humanoid robot developed by the Hong Kong-based company Hanson Robotics. Sophia was activated on February 14, 2016, and made her first public appearance in mid-March 2016 at South by Southwest (SXSW) in Austin, Texas, United States. Sophia was marketed as a "social robot" who can mimic social behaviour and induce feelings of love in humans. Sophia has been covered by media around the globe, and has participated in many high-profile interviews. In October 2017, Sophia was granted Saudi Arabian citizenship, becoming the first robot to receive legal personhood in any country. In November 2017, Sophia was named the United Nations Development Programme's first Innovation Champion, and is the first non-human to be given a United Nations title. According to founder David Hanson, Sophia's source code is about 70% open source. A paper describing of one of Sophia's open-source subsystems, called "Open Arms", was submitted to 36th Conference on Neural Information Processing Systems (NeurIPS 2022)

SENSORS

Custom wide-angle 1080p chest camera. Intel RealSense camera. Two custom 720p HD cameras (one for each eye).

External USB microphone. Joint angle sensors and force sensors in arm joints. Touch sensors in fingers. Audio localization array. Inertial measurement unit (IMU).

ACTUATORS

Head and face: Five Dynamixel XM430 servos and 23 Xpert servos. Eyes: Two Hitec HS-65MG servos. Neck: Three Dynamixel XM430 servos. Arms and hands: Two Dynamixel MX64 servos, one Dynamixel MX106 servo, four Dynamixel XM430 servos, six Xpert servos, and two MKS servos (per arm/hand).

DEGREES OF FREEDOM (DOF)

83 (Head and neck: 36 DoF; Arm and hand: 15 DoF x 2; Torso: 3 DoF; Mobile base: 14 DoF)

MATERIALS

Frubber (actuated skin), carbon fiber, CNC aluminum, steel, Spectra fiber, Delrin thermoplastic, acrylic, polycarbonate, 3D-printed parts, and other mixed media.

COMPUTE: -3 GHz Intel i7 with 32 GB RAM, integrated GPU

SOFTWARE: -Ubuntu Linux OS, Ethernet, Wi-Fi

POWER: - 110/220-V power supply or 24-V lithium-polymer battery.

Sophia

8.Metaverse-Technology

The metaverse is the emerging 3-D-enabled digital space that uses virtual reality, augmented reality, and other advanced internet and semiconductor technology to allow people to have lifelike personal and business experiences online.

he metaverse is having a moment: if you've ever done a Google search for the term "metaverse," you're not alone. In 2021, internet searches for the term increased by 7,200 percent. And once people get the gist, most of them are all in: recent McKinsey research shows that approximately 60 percent of consumers are excited about the transition of everyday activities like shopping, dating, and working out to the metaverse. But it's not just individuals who are meta-curious: private capital is betting big money on the metaverse. In 2021, metaverse-related companies reportedly raised more than $10 billion, more than twice what they did in 2020. And so far in 2022, more than $120 billion has flowed into the metaverse. The latest McKinsey research shows that the metaverse has the potential to generate up to $5 trillion in value by 2030. It's an opportunity that is too big to ignore. The metaverse means different things to different people. Some believe it's a digital playground for friends. Others think it has the potential to be a commercial space for companies and customers. We believe both interpretations are correct. In June 2022, McKinsey released Value creation in the metaverse, a new report based on surveys of more than 3,400 consumers and executives, as well as interviews with 13 senior leaders and metaverse experts. Based on this analysis, we believe the metaverse is best characterized as an evolution of today's internet—something we are deeply immersed in, rather than something we primarily look at. It represents a convergence of digital technology to combine and extend the reach and use of cryptocurrency, artificial intelligence (AI), augmented reality (AR) and virtual reality (VR), spatial computing, and more. And the "enterprise metaverse" may coalesce in a way that unlocks even more opportunity, beyond simply serving as a virtual place where people interact. At its most basic, the metaverse will have three features: 1.A sense of immersion 2. Real-time interactivity 3. User agency

And ultimately, the full vision of the metaverse will include the following:

platforms and devices that work seamlessly with each other, the possibility for thousands of people to interact simultaneously, use cases well beyond gaming the metaverse isn't about escaping reality, says futurist Cathy Hackl. Instead, it's about "embracing and augmenting it with virtual content and experiences that can make things more fulfilling and make us feel more connected to our loved ones, more productive at work, and happier." For Brian Solis, Salesforce's global innovation evangelist, "what the metaverse is really all about is community. The value of belonging to this community. The role you can play as a user in this community so that you feel like a stakeholder and not a 'user.'"

Metaverse-Pic

9.AI Replicated Evaluation & Created Original Proteins

Scientists have created an AI "Pyrogen" capable of generating artificial enzymes from scratch. The tool managed to design anti- microbial proteins that ware able to work in real life. Scientists say that this could be used to create new medicines.

In laboratory tests, some of these enzymes worked as well as those found in nature, even when their artificially generated amino acid sequences diverged significantly from any known natural protein The experiment demonstrates that natural language processing, though developed to read and write language text, can learn at least some of the underlying principles of biology. Salesforce Research developed the AI program, called pyrogen, which uses next-token prediction to assemble amino acid sequences into artificial proteins. Scientists said the new technology could become more powerful than directed evolution, a Nobel-prize-winning protein design technology, and will energize the 50-year-old field of protein engineering by speeding the development of new proteins that can be used for almost anything from therapeutics to degrading plastic.

How It Works: - A user enters a control tag, which can be a protein type such as lysosome, into the pyrogen AI model. The pyrogen AI model uses the tag to assemble amino acid sequences into artificial proteins. These new artificial proteins can be used for almost anything from therapeutics to degrading plastic. To create the model, scientists simply fed the amino acid sequences of 280 million different proteins of all kinds into the machine learning model and let it digest the information for a couple of weeks. Then, they fine-tuned the model by priming it with 56,000 sequences from five lysozyme families, along with some contextual information about these proteins. The model quickly generated a million sequences, and the research team selected 100 to test based on how closely they resembled the sequences of natural proteins. Ref source: Nature Biotechnology

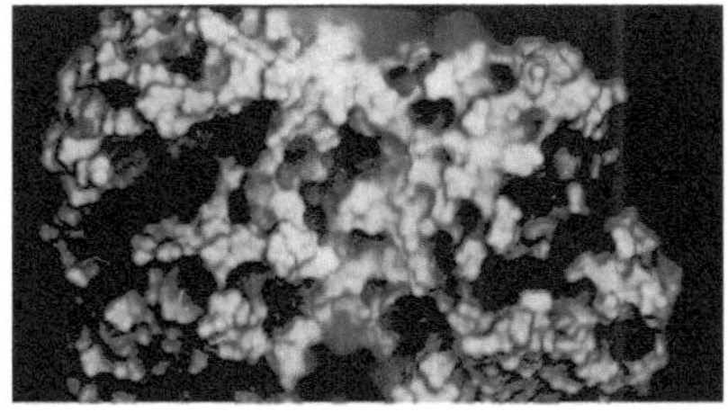

Proteins

10. Google's New AI Can Turn Any Text into Music

*Google has announced an AI tool" MusicLM "that has the capability of **turning words into music**. It can also transform whistled & hummed melodies according to the style described in a text caption. MusicLM was trained on a dataset of **280,000 hours of music.***

Researchers at Google have revealed a text-to-music AI that creates songs that can last as long as five minutes.

Releasing a paper with their work and findings so far, the team introduced MusicLM to the world with a number of examples that do bear a surprising resemblance to their text prompts.

The researchers claim their model "outperforms previous systems both in audio quality and adherence to the text description". Using AI to generate music is nothing new - but a tool that can actually generate passable music based on a simple text prompt has yet to be showcased yet. That is until now, according to the team behind MusicLM. The model also allows for audio input, in the form of whistling or humming for example, to help to inform the melody of the song, which will then be "rendered in the style described by the text prompt".

It has not yet been released to the public, with the authors acknowledging the risks of potential "misappropriation of creative content" should a generated song not differ sufficiently from the source material the model learned from.

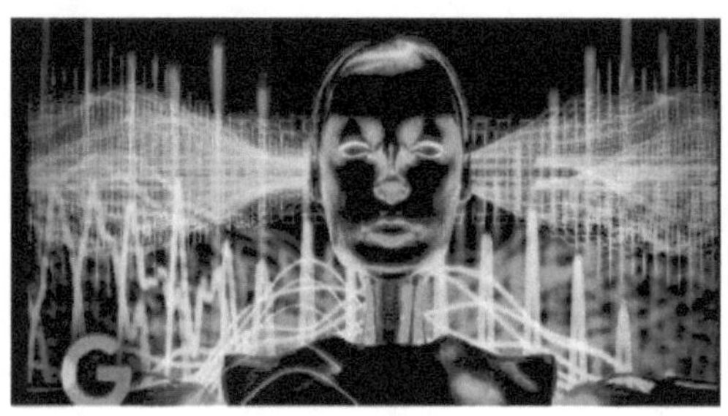

Google's New AI

11. Meet Aiko and Aiden, The World's First AI Interns.

AI Interns, *named Aiko and Aiden, joined a team of 106 people at a US-based marketing under their assigned reporting Managers. If their internship is successful, they will be getting **a full-time role.***

Codeword, a leading tech-marketing agency, has hired the world's first AI interns.

The interns named Aiden and Aiko have been hired for a three-month trial internship and will be working alongside Codeword's team of 106 people.

Aiko will work on Codeword's design team, while Aiden will work with the company's editorial team. They will be given internal creative assignments, share their experiences on the company's blog and social media accounts, and even get regular performance evaluations during their three-month internship. The interns will be assigned work by the team and they will work towards identifying their skills and nurture them through the internship as they progress to a potential full-time role. Codeword will monitor their progress and output regularly. Though they are not expected to produce client-facing work, They will be required to produce the nature of creative work AI is skilled at which may include handling and managing content at scale or even generating large volumes of rough concept thumbnails for mood boards, analyzing trends and news, etc for the editorial team. Aiden will be a part of an editorial team spanning over 30 writers and editors. Aiko will join the design team, which includes graphic designers, videographers, animators, UX designers, and front-end developers.

12.ChatGPT Has Managed to Pass the US Medical Exam

*ChatGPT and its use cases remain a fascinating topic in the tech world. Now, ChatGPT managed to pass **the US Medical Licensing Examination**, an exam that is typically given by medical students hoping to become licensing doctors.*

In fact, as researchers showed in one paper ChatGPT passed the exam which includes three steps for various levels of medical professionals but also offered insights and explanations for how it arrived at its answers. The first paper, which was published in December, and is available for reading on medRxivopens, showed that ChatGPT was able to achieve more than 50 percent accuracy across all of the exams. These results suggest that large language models may have the potential to assist with medical education, and potentially, clinical decision-making. In another interesting case, ChatGPT has managed to pass an MBA exam designed by a professor of Wharton from the University of Pennsylvania. The ChatGPT-3 powered chatbot has passed the final exam of the MBA course scoring between a B- and B grade. According to the report, the ChatGPT bot has an "amazing job at basic operations management and process analysis questions including those that are based on case studies," with excellent explanation. The bot was also said to be good at "modifying its answers in response to human hints."

According to educators, ChatGPT's response style makes it difficult to distinguish it from human responses. Experts in artificial intelligence and educators suggest that products like ChatGPT might pose a negative effect on the education system in the future while some are not at all concerned about it. Ref: MSN; Business Today

13. A New Space Race? NASA Administrator Is Worried!

*According to NASA's top administrator **Bill Nelson,** China space race. He warned that if China prevails, it may claim ownership of **territory on the moon.** China is planning to build a **lunar base by 2030s.***

NASA Administrator Bill Nelson claims that the U.S. is in a space race with China which could see Beijing attempt to make territorial claims to parts of the moon. Both China and the United States have lofty goals for lunar exploration and colonization. Both the U.S. and China have major lunar ambitions, with NASA working on its Artemis program to return astronauts to the moon, while China aims to send its own crews to the moon before the end of the decade and build a lunar base in the 2030s. Both powers are considering landing in some of the same areas near the lunar south pole. "It is a fact: we're in a space race," the NASA administrator said in an interview. "And it is true that we better watch out that they don't get to a place on the moon under the guise of scientific research. And it is not beyond the realm of possibility that they say, 'Keep out, we're here, this is our territory.'"

Still, there is no legal basis for claiming territory in space. China, like the U.S. and 132 other countries, is a signatory to the 1967 Outer Space Treaty, which states that "Outer space, including the moon and other celestial bodies, is not subject to national appropriation by claim of sovereignty, by means of use or occupation, or by any other means." Nelson, however, points to Chinese behavior and territorial claims in the South China Sea as a possible indicator of future claims being made on the moon. Chinese space industry figures have moved to refute Nelson's latest claims.

14. Researchers Simulated a Synthetic Block Hole in Lab

A team from the University of Amsterdam in the Netherlands simulated the event horizon of a black hole in a lab and observed the equivalent of an elusive form of radiation first theorized by Stephen Hawking.

The new discovery could help the scientific community develop a whole new theory that marries the general theory of relativity with the principles of quantum mechanics. In

1974, Stephen Hawking proposed that interruptions to quantum fluctuations caused by the event horizon result in a type of radiation very similar to thermal radiation.

If this Hawking radiation exists, it's way too faint for us to detect yet. It's possible we'll never sift it out of the hissing static of the Universe. But we can probe its properties by creating black hole analogs in laboratory settings. A one-dimensional chain of atoms served as a path for electrons to 'hop' from one position to another. By tuning the ease with which this hopping can occur, the physicists could cause certain properties to vanish, effectively creating a kind of event horizon that interfered with the wave-like nature of the electrons.

The effect of this fake event horizon produced a rise in temperature that matched theoretical expectations of an equivalent black hole system, but only when part of the chain extended beyond the event horizon. This could mean the entanglement of particles that straddle the event horizon is instrumental in generating Hawking radiation.

15. Microrobots Can Now Swim & Navigate Using AI

Researchers taught smart microrobots how to swim & navigate with AI. These micro swimmers could learn and adapt to changing conditions through AI and can be used for targeted drug delivery and microsurgery.

Researchers from Santa Clara University, New Jersey Institute of Technology, and the University of Hong Kong have been able to successfully teach microrobots how to swim via deep reinforcement learning, marking a substantial leap in the progression of micro swimming capability.

The microswimmers could learn and adapt to changing conditions through AI. Much like humans (learning to swim) require reinforcement learning and feedback to stay afloat and propel in various directions under changing conditions, so too must microswimmers, though with their unique set of challenges imposed by physics in the microscopic world. The team successfully taught a simple micro swimmer to swim and navigate in any arbitrary direction by combining artificial neural networks with reinforcement learning. When the swimmer moves in certain ways, it receives feedback on how good the particular action is. The swimmer then progressively learns how to swim based on its experiences interacting with the surrounding environment. "Similar to a human learning how to swim, the micro swimmer learns how to move its body parts – in this case, three microparticles and extensible links – to self-propel and turn," said Alan Tsang, assistant professor of mechanical engineering at the University of Hong Kong. "It does so without relying on human knowledge but only on a machine learning algorithm." During the tests, the researchers showed that it could follow a complex path without being explicitly programmed. They also demonstrated the robust performance of the smart microrobots in navigating under the perturbations arising from external fluid flows.

TWO
SPACE TECHNOLOGY

1.Scientists Manipulated Quantum Light, At the First Time

A single photon has confirmed Einstein's theory of stimulated emission. Scientists have now discovered and controlled individual photons, which has made it possible to control quantum light.

Scientists have been able to recognize and control small quantities of interacting photons, or light energy packets, with success. The group claims that this study is a historically significant breakthrough for quantum technologies.

The laser was invented on the basis of stimulated light emission, a theory first put out by Einstein in 1916 that explains how photons can cause atoms to produce more photons (Light Amplification by Stimulated Emission of Radiation). Although stimulated emission has long been known to occur for huge numbers of photons, this new research has made it possible for scientists to detect and control single photon stimulated emission for the first time. One photon and two bound photons scattering off a single quantum dot—a kind of artificially manufactured atom—were subjected to a direct time delay measurement. According to Sahand Mahmoodian, a co-lead author of a study report from the University of Sydney School of Physics, "this opens the door to the manipulation of what we can call 'quantum light.'" Researchers continue to find chances to find real-world applications based on theoretical knowledge of the interaction between light and matter, from medical imaging to computers and GPS to communication networking. For example, in communication, photons that are difficult to interact with one another can be utilized to transport information nearly distortion-free and at the speed of light.

It is desirable for light to interact with other light, though, sometimes. And on a quantum level of a single photon, which has long baffled scientists. Researchers employed a novel apparatus to create intense interactions between photons in order to finally understand how it functions and make it happen. This device allowed the team to see the difference in time delay between one photon bouncing off a quantum dot and a bound pair of photons doing the same thing.

Implications: This breakthrough opens the door to advances in quantum-enhanced measurement techniques and photonic quantum computing. It represents a fundamental step forward in the field of quantum technologies, potentially leading to new applications we can't yet fully imagine.

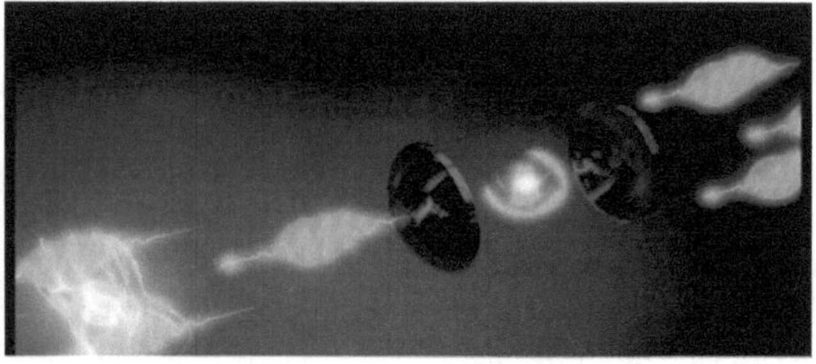

Quantum Light

2. This Could Create the First-Ever Traversable Wormhole

A new experiment by physicists at the University of Bristol's Quantum Engineering Technology Labs could lead to the first-ever traversable wormhole and enable a form of teleportation that they have named "counterrotation." Scientists Are Preparing to Create a Traversable Quantum Wormhole!

Although wormholes are popular in science fiction and research studies, no one has ever produced a real one in an experiment or even identified one in the universe.

This may all change as Hatim Salih, a quantum physicist at the University of Bristol's Quantum Engineering Technology Labs, has devised a way to achieve this out-of-reach goal. "Imagine if someone's consciousness, like a strong AI, is copied into a quantum object," Salih said.

"If you counter port each one the quits, transport them from one place to another—and if this thing has a subjective experience—then it possibly could tell you what it feels like to go through a wormhole."

He plans to engineer a first-of-its-kind traversable wormhole with a special kind of quantum computer. "The key thing is it uses current technology and currently available components," added Salih. "The hope is that within the next three to four years, we will have built this thing." At the basis of the new experiment lies a principle coined as "counterrotation" by Salih. The word emerged from combining "counterfactual" and "transportation."

Counterrotation would allow scientists to send light through a quantum wormhole system frozen in an "off" state by constant observation. Meanwhile, at the wormhole's other end, scientists could reconstruct the light without any electricity or particles ever being sent.

"Counterrotation gives you the end goal of the object being reconstituted across space, but we can verify that nothing has passed," Salih explained.

"This is key for other important considerations or consequences because if we can strictly say nothing has passed, then we can examine some questions in physics, for example, afresh in a different light."

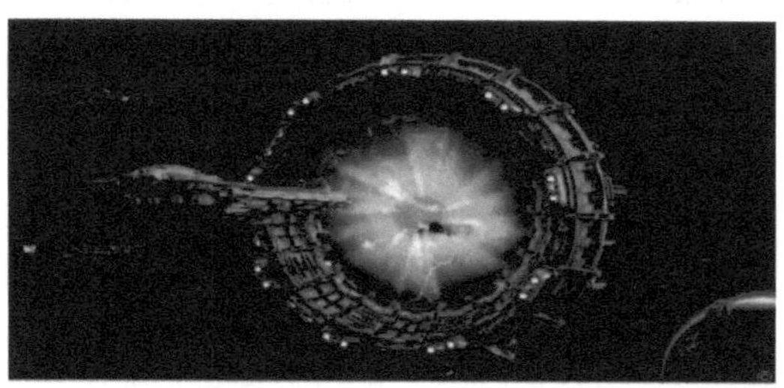

Traversable Wormhole

3.Scientists Creates Cosmic Concrete for Mars Settlers.

Scientists have created a new material, dubbed 'Star Crete' which is made from extra-terrestrial dust, potato starch, and a pinch of salt and could be used to build homes on Mars.

This material is twice as strong as ordinary concrete. Building infrastructure in space is currently prohibitively expensive and difficult to achieve. Future space construction will need to rely on simple materials that are easily available to astronauts, Star Crete offers one possible solution. The scientists behind the invention used simulated Martian soil mixed with potato starch and a pinch of salt to create a material that is twice as strong as ordinary concrete and is perfectly suited for construction work in extra-terrestrial environments. In an article published in the journal Open Engineering, the University of Manchester research team demonstrated that ordinary potato starch can act as a binder when mixed with simulated Mars dust to produce a concrete-like material.

When tested, Star Crete had a compressive strength of 72 Megapascals (MPa), which is over twice as strong as the 32 MPa seen in ordinary concrete. Star Crete made from moon dust was even stronger at over 91 MPa.

This work improves on previous work from the same team where they used astronauts' blood and urine as a binding agent. While the resulting material had a compressive strength of around 40 MPa, which is better than normal concrete, the process had the drawback of requiring blood regularly. When operating in an environment as hostile as space, this option was seen as less feasible than using potato starch. "Since we will be producing starch as food for astronauts, it made sense to look at that as a binding agent rather than human blood. Also, current building technologies still need many years of development and require considerable energy and additional heavy processing equipment which all add cost and complexity to a mission. Star Crete doesn't need any of this and so it simplifies the mission and makes it cheaper and more feasible.

Cosmic Concrete

4. There May Have Been a Second Big Bang: Study

Within a month of the Big Bang, a second cosmic explosion may have given the universe its invisible dark matter, new research suggests. We may be able to see the evidence for that event by studying ripples in the fabric of space-time.

The Big Bang may have been accompanied by a shadow, the "Dark" Big Bang that flooded our cosmos with mysterious dark matter, cosmologists have proposed in a new study.

After the Big Bang, most cosmologists think, the universe underwent a period of rapid, remarkable expansion in its earliest moments, known as inflation.

Nobody knows what triggered inflation, but it's necessary to explain a variety of observations, like the extreme geometrical flatness of the universe at large scales. Inflation was presumably driven by some exotic quantum field, which is a fundamental entity that soaks all of spacetime. At the end of inflation, that field decayed into a shower of particles and radiation, triggering the "Hot Big Bang" those physicists commonly associate with the beginning of the universe.

Those particles would go on to coalesce into the first atoms when the cosmos was around 12 minutes old and — hundreds of millions of years later — begin clumping into stars and galaxies. But there's another ingredient to the cosmological mix: dark matter. Once again, cosmologists aren't sure what dark matter is, but they see the evidence for its existence through its gravitational influence on normal matter.

In the simplest models, the end of inflation and the ensuing Hot Big Bang also flooded the universe with dark matter, which evolved along an independent track. But this assumption is made merely for the sake of simplicity, as two cosmologists proposed in a paper.

Scientists see no evidence for the existence of dark matter until far later in the evolution of the universe, after the elusive substance had enough time to exert gravitational influence, so there's no need for it to have filled the universe in the Hot Big Bang alongside normal matter. Plus, because dark matter does not interact with normal matter, it might have had its own "Dark" Big Bang, the researchers claim.

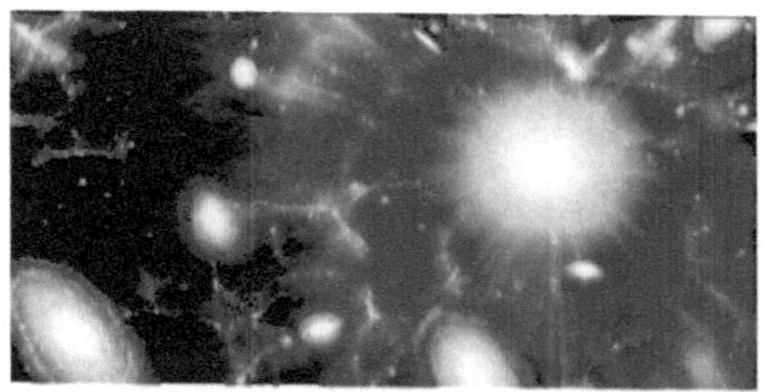

Second Big Bang

5.First Detailed Map of Water Distribution on The Moon

We finally have a map of water spread on the Moon that will guide future crewed missions, including Artemis III. Scientists used data from NASA's retired SOFIA telescope to compile the first detailed map of lunar water distribution.

A new study using the now-retired Stratospheric Observatory for Infrared Astronomy (SOFIA) has pieced together the first detailed, wide-area map of water distribution on the Moon. The new map covers about one-quarter of the Earth-facing side of the lunar surface below 60 degrees latitude and extends to the Moon's South Pole.
In this data visualization, SOFIA's lunar water observations are indicated using color, with blue representing areas of higher water signal, and brown less. With clear, identifiable lunar features marked out by the water data, the study provides hints about how water may be moving across the Moon's surface, particularly near its South Pole — an important area for space exploration. Given the large region covered, the researchers could easily identify how water relates to surface features on the Moon, staying away

from sunlight and favoring cold areas. "When looking at the water data, we can actually see crater rims, we see the individual mountains, and we can even see differences between the day and night sides of the mountains, thanks to the higher concentration of water in these places," said Bill Reach, director of the SOFIA Science Center at NASA's Ames Research Center in California's Silicon Valley and lead author on the study, which was presented at the 2023 Lunar and Planetary Science Conference.

In late 2024, NASA's Volatiles Investigating Polar Exploration Rover (VIPER) will land in the region studied by SOFIA, atop Mons Mouton, to conduct the first resource mapping mission beyond Earth. The flat-topped lunar mountain will be a region of emphasis in the next paper from the team that led the current study of SOFIA data. Ref: NASA

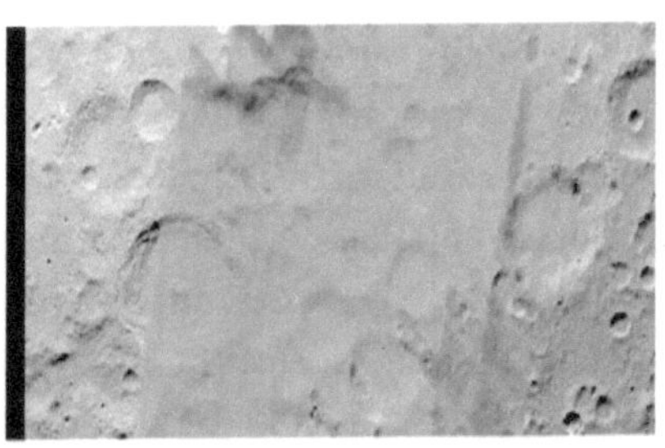

Moon Surface

6. Earth's Water Is Officially Older Than the Sun

Astronomers found a link between water from the interstellar medium and the water here on earth, showing a few chemical

similarities. This research indicates that water in our Solar system is billions of years older than the sun.

Astronomers found a link Between water from the interstellar Scientists looking into the origin of life on Earth have claimed that the water present on the planet is very, very old. In fact, a new study has said that it's older than the Sun.

The research is based on the discovery of water vapor around V883 Orionis, a young star, 1,305 light years away from Earth. Scientists said that the water surrounding the star has the same chemical markers as water on Earth. They added this supports the idea that water on Earth is even older than our Sun. "We can now trace the origins of water in our Solar System to before the formation of the Sun," said John J Tobin, an astronomer at the National Radio Astronomy Observatory in the US, and lead author of the study published in Nature. The space scientists used Atacama Large Millimeter Array (ALMA) to measure chemical signatures of the water and its path from the star-forming cloud to the planets, according to a release by European Southern Observatory (ESO). "The composition of the water in the disc is very similar to that of comets in our own Solar System. This is confirmation of the idea that the water in planetary systems formed billions of years ago, before the Sun, in interstellar space, and has been inherited by both comets and Earth, relatively unchanged," Mr. Tobin added. Researchers have so far said that comets delivered water to Earth. They found the water from clouds to stars and then from comets to planets, but the link between the young stars and comets was missing.

Ref: Nature Journal; National Radio Astronomy Observatory

Sun/Earth

7.Astronomers Discover the Oldest Known Black Hole, Breaking a Record Set Last Year:

The supermassive structure dates to about 400 million years after the Big Bang, and it's particularly large for its age

Astronomers using the James Webb Space Telescope (JWST) have detected the earliest known black hole. Located more than 13 billion light-years away, it dates to a mere 400 million years after the Big Bang. The black hole lies at the center of a galaxy called GN-z11, which, at the time of its discovery in 2016, was the oldest galaxy ever spotted. But what has shocked researchers about this early black hole is its large size. "It's not its age that is surprising, it is the fact that it is already so big so early in the universe, which is difficult to explain with standard theories," Roberto Maiolino, a co-author of the study and astrophysicist at the University of Cambridge in the United Kingdom, tells Newsweek's Jess Thomson. Black holes are incomprehensible quantities of matter stuffed into a relatively small space. Because they're so dense, their gravitational pull is powerful enough to suck in anything that comes close, including light. As a result, black holes can't be observed directly—scientists can only see their effect on their surroundings. In the case of the galaxy GN-z11, researchers had already noticed it was unusually bright. To be so luminous, "it would have required a large number of stars packed in such a small volume," Maiolino tells NPR's Ari Daniel.

But observations from Webb revealed the galaxy's bright light doesn't come from stars—instead, it's from hot gas swirling around the black hole as it gets sucked inside. "These authors have made a persuasive case that there is a black hole," Priyamvada Natarajan, an astrophysicist at Yale University who did not contribute to the findings, tells NPR. In November, Natarajan and other astronomers announced the discovery of what was, at the time, the earliest known black hole, dating to 470 million years after the Big Bang. The Webb telescope played a role in that discovery as well. That black hole was also unexpectedly massive—between 10 million and 100 million times the mass of our sun. "It's just really early on in the universe to be such a behemoth," Natarajan told Marcia Dunn of the Associated Press at the time. The newly discovered black hole is roughly 1.6 million times as massive as our sun, according to Live Science's Ben Turner. Scientists previously thought that black holes gradually grew to the massive sizes they are today, according to a statement from the University of Cambridge. But if the newly discovered black hole had grown according to the standard models, it would take about a billion years to reach its large size. So, for the object to be as big as it is during the young universe, it would have had to either start out much larger than thought or grow much more quickly than expected. "This black hole is essentially eating the [equivalent of] an entire sun every five years," Maiolino tells NPR. "It's actually much higher than we thought could be feasible for these black holes." According to the leading theories, for early black holes to become so massive that quickly, they might have formed from the sudden collapse of giant gas clouds or from many stars and black holes merging together. "Understanding where the black holes came from in the first place has always been a puzzle, but now that puzzle seems to be deepening," Andrew Pontzen, a cosmologist at University College London who was not involved in the research, told the Guardian's Hannah Devlin in December, when the paper was published as a preprint. "These results, using the power of JWST to peer back through time, suggest that some black

holes instead grew at a tremendous rate in the young universe, far faster than we expected."

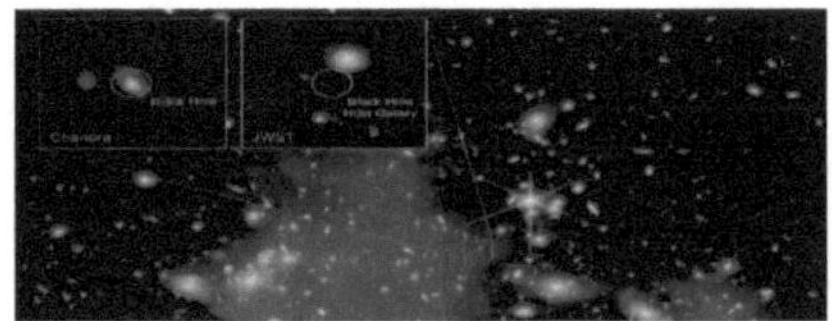

GN-z11

8. Earth Will Continue to Warm and the Effects Will Be Profound

The magnitude and rate of climate change and associated risks depend strongly on near-term mitigation and adaptation actions, and projected adverse impacts and related losses and damages escalate with every increment of global warming.

Global climate change is not a future problem. Changes to Earth's climate driven by increased human emissions of heat-trapping greenhouse gases are already having widespread effects on the environment: glaciers and ice sheets are shrinking, river and lake ice is breaking up earlier, plant and animal geographic ranges are shifting, and plants and trees are blooming sooner. Effects that scientists had long predicted would result from global climate change are now occurring, such as sea ice loss, accelerated sea level rise, and longer, more intense heat waves. Some changes (such as droughts, wildfires, and extreme rainfall) are happening faster than scientists previously assessed. In fact, according to the Intergovernmental Panel on Climate Change (IPCC) — the United Nations body established to assess the science related to climate change — modern humans have never before seen the observed changes in our global climate, and some of these changes are irreversible over the next hundreds to thousands of years. Scientists have high confidence that global temperatures will continue to rise for many decades, mainly due to greenhouse gases produced by human activities. The IPCC's Sixth Assessment report, published in 2021, found that human emissions of heat-trapping gases have already warmed the climate by nearly 2 degrees Fahrenheit (1.1 degrees Celsius) since 1850-1900. The global average temperature is expected to reach or exceed 1.5 degrees C (about 3 degrees F) within the next few decades. These changes will affect all regions of Earth. The severity of effects caused by climate change will depend on the path of future human activities. More greenhouse gas emissions will lead to more climate extremes and widespread damaging effects across our planet. However, those future effects depend on the total amount of carbon dioxide we emit. So, if we can reduce emissions, we may avoid some of the worst effects. The scientific evidence is unequivocal: climate change is a threat to human wellbeing and the health of the planet. Any further delay in concerted global action will miss the brief, rapidly closing window to secure a liveable future.

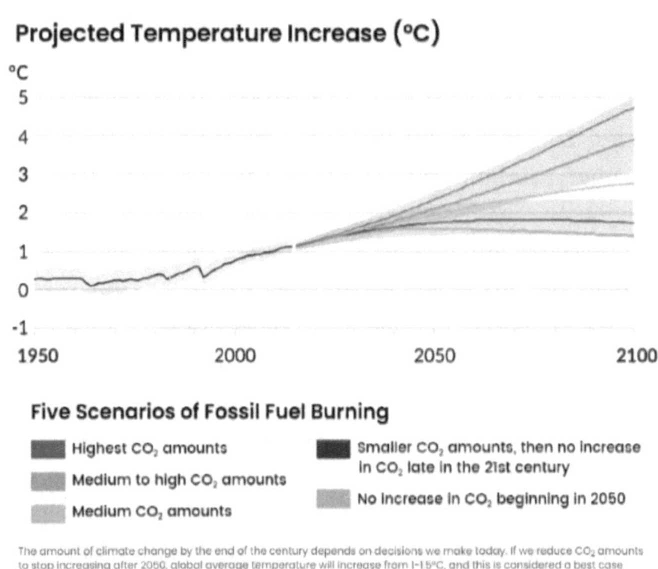

The amount of climate change by the end of the century depends on decisions we make today. If we reduce CO₂ amounts to stop increasing after 2050, global average temperature will increase from 1–1.5°C, and this is considered a best case scenario (blue line in graph). If we don't reduce CO₂ and the amounts continue to increase, the worst case scenario warming will be 4.5–5°C (red line in graph).

IPCC Working Group I, 2021

Predictions of Future Global Climate

Scientists from around the world serve as part of the Intergovernmental Panel on Climate Change (IPCC). These scientists have found that from 1900-2020, the world's surface air temperature increased an average of 1.1° Celsius (nearly 2°F) due to burning fossil fuels that releases carbon dioxide and other greenhouse gases into the atmosphere.

This may not sound like very much change, but this warming is unprecedented in over 2000 years of records. Even one degree can impact the planet in many ways. Climate models predict that Earth's global average temperature will rise an additional 4° C (7.2° F) during the 21st Century if greenhouse gas levels continue to rise at present levels. Without swift action to reduce greenhouse gas emissions, models project that holding global average temperatures to within a 1.5-2.0°C (2.7-3.6°F) increase may no longer be possible.

Predicted Impacts of Climate Change

Climate change is predicted to impact regions differently. For example, temperature increases are expected to be greater on land than over oceans and greater at high latitudes than in the tropics and mid-latitudes. Warmer temperatures will cause (and are causing) changes to other aspects of climate - such as rain, snow, and clouds. They are also causing changes to the ocean, life, ice, and all other parts of the Earth system.

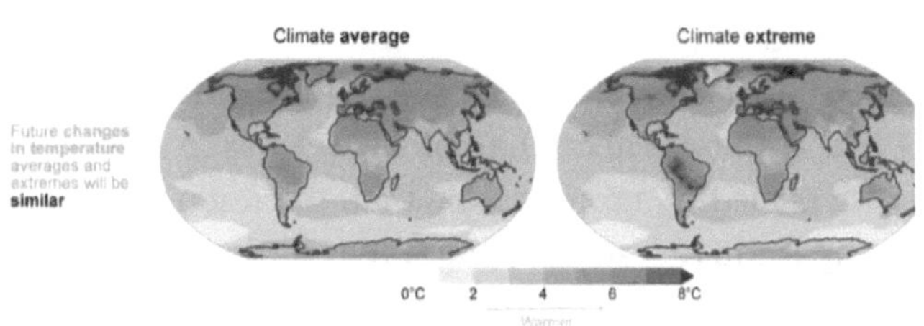

Warming is already occurring in all areas of the globe, but models of future temperatures show that the changes will not be distributed equally. Polar regions and land areas are expected to see the largest temperature changes.
IPCC Working Group I, 2021

Changing Precipitation

A warmer average global temperature will cause the water cycle to "speed up" due to a higher rate of evaporation. More water vapor in the atmosphere will lead to more precipitation. Global average precipitation can increase by 7% for each degree of warming, which means we are looking at a future with much more rain and snow, and a higher risk of flooding to some regions. With a 2°C temperature increase, heavy rain events are expected to become 1.7 times more likely, and 14% more intense. However, changes in precipitation will not be evenly distributed. Some locations will get more, and others will see less.

Melting Snow and Ice

As the climate warms, snow and ice melt. It is predicted that the melting of glaciers, ice sheets, and other snow and ice on land in the summer will continue to be greater than the amount of precipitation that falls in the winter, which means a decrease in the total amount of snow and ice on the planet. Over the past 100 years, mountain glaciers in all areas of the world have decreased in size and so has the amount of permafrost in the Arctic. Greenland's ice sheet is melting faster, too. The amount of sea ice (frozen seawater) floating in the Arctic Ocean and around Antarctica is expected to decrease. Already the summer thickness of sea ice in the Arctic is about half of what it was in 1950. Arctic sea ice is melting more rapidly than the Antarctic Sea ice. Melting ice may lead to changes in ocean circulation, too. Although there is some uncertainty about the amount of melt, summer in the Arctic Ocean will likely be ice-free by the end of the century.

Rising Sea Level

A warmer climate causes sea level to rise via two mechanisms: (1) melting glaciers and ice sheets (ice on land) add water to the oceans, raising the sea level, and (2) ocean water expands as it warms, increasing its volume and thus also raising sea level. Since 1880, sea levels have risen about 0.10 to 0.20 meters (0.3 to 0.75 feet) depending on region and location. Thermal expansion and melting ice each contributed about half of the rise, though there is some uncertainty in the exact magnitude of the contribution from each source. By the year 2050, models predict sea level will rise an additional 0.25 to 0.30 meters, and by 2100, without immediate reductions in greenhouse gas emissions, global sea level rise is expected to be on the order of 1.1 meters (3.5 feet). Some low-lying areas could experience even higher levels, threatening coastal communities, wetlands, and global trade. Even if swift emission reductions occur, the greenhouse gases levels currently present will still likely result in about 0.6 meters (2 feet) of sea level rise by the end of the century.

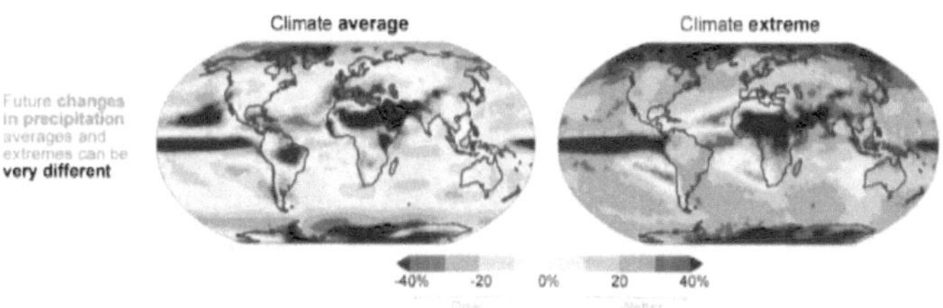

Future changes in precipitation will vary regionally, with some parts of the globe likely to become wetter and other areas projected to become drier.
IPCC Working Group I, 2021

Acidic Ocean Water

Earth's oceans are predicted to act as a buffer against climate change by taking up some of the excess heat and carbon dioxide from the atmosphere. This is good news in the short run, but more problematic in the long run. Carbon dioxide combined with seawater forms weak carbonic acid. Scientists believe this process has reduced the pH of the oceans by about 0.1 pH since pre-industrial times. Further acidification of 0.14 to 0.35 pH is expected by the year 2100. Higher acidity in the ocean causes problems for coral reefs and other marine organisms.

Changes to Ocean Currents

Large-scale ocean currents called thermohaline circulation, driven by differences in salinity and temperature, may also be disrupted as the climate warms. Changes in precipitation patterns and the influx of fresh water into the oceans from melting ice can alter salinity. Changing salinity, along with rising water temperature, may disrupt the currents. In an extreme case, thermohaline circulation could be disrupted or even shut down in some parts of the ocean, which could have large effects on climate.

Changing Severe Weather

Some climate scientists believe that hurricanes, typhoons, and other tropical cyclones will change as a result of global warming. Warm ocean surface waters provide the energy that drives these immense storms. Warmer oceans in the future are expected to cause the intensification of such storms. Although there may not be more tropical cyclones worldwide in the future, some scientists believe there will be a higher proportion of the most powerful and destructive storms. Some scientists believe we already see evidence for an upswing in the numbers of the most powerful storms. Others are less convinced.

Changing Clouds

Clouds are a bit of a wild card in global climate models. Warmer global temperatures produce faster overall evaporation rates, resulting in more water vapor in the atmosphere...and more clouds. Different types of clouds at different locations have different effects on climate. Some shade the Earth, cooling the climate. Others enhance the greenhouse effect with their heat-trapping water vapor and droplets. Scientists expect a warmer world to be a cloudier one, but are not yet certain how the increased cloudiness will feed back into the climate system. Modelling the influence of clouds in the climate system is an area of active scientific research.

Risks to Marine Life

Ocean ecosystems will change as sea-surface temperatures continues to warm. Animals like fish are able to move to other ecosystems with cooler water at higher latitudes. But many marine organisms – like kelp and corals – that aren't able to swim elsewhere are at high risk. Warmer waters in the shallow oceans have contributed to the death of about a quarter of the world's coral reefs in the last few decades. Many of the coral animals died after being weakened by bleaching, a process tied to warmed waters.

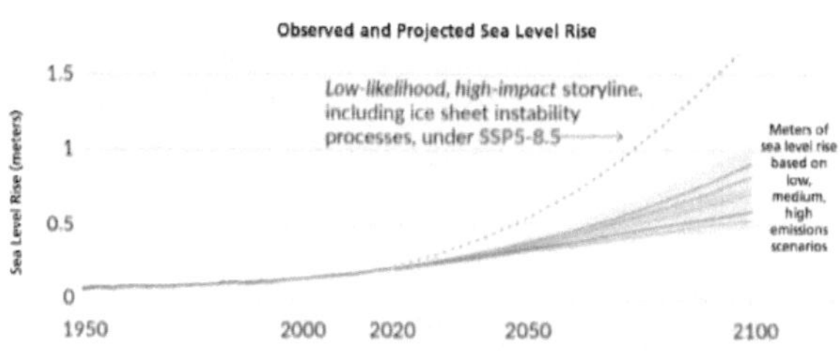

Observed (black line) and projected sea level rise through 2100, where the colored curves indicate sea level rise for different emissions scenarios.
IPCC Sixth Assessment Report

Risks to Life on Land

Changes in temperature, precipitation, and seasonal timing will alter the geographic ranges of many types of plants and animals. Since species can only survive if they are in a habitat that suits their needs, many species will face extinction if the geographic range where they can survive shrinks. If warming is kept to 2°C, 18% of insects, 16% of plants, and 8% of vertebrate animals are projected to lose over half of their geographic range. However, if we can keep the amount of warming to 1.5°C, the habitat loss to insects, plants, and vertebrates decreases by about a half. On the other hand, the range of some species, such as mosquitos which carry different types of diseases, may increase due to climate warming. Warming surface temperatures are also predicted to increase the frequency of heat waves and droughts, which can affect crop production, increase the risk of wildfires, and even impact human health.

9. NASA Plans to Use Lasers to Remove Space Junk

NASA is considering using ground & space-based laser to remove space debris in Earth's orbit, as experts estimates 100 trillion pieces of junk are lingering in space and endangering satellites. The other methods proposed including tugs.

Removing space debris is necessary because junk in Earth's orbit poses a threat to orbiting satellites and outgoing spacecraft, NASA said, as an estimated $23 million in damage could be averted each time 100,000 pieces of small debris (measured between 1 and 10 centimeters) are removed. NASA's 147-page report assesses numerous options but does not indicate which method is preferred, though it does specify its preference for the use of ground- or space-based lasers for smaller debris and space tugs for larger debris.

NASA suggests efforts to alleviate the issue could "achieve net benefits in under a decade" after a method is decided on—which would require cooperation with the U.S. government and military, the agency noted.

While it is difficult to quantify the space debris risk (as not all pieces are trackable), humanity has sent more than 15,000 satellites aloft since the first 1957 launch of the Soviet Union's Sputnik, and only about 7,200 of that number are operational, according to the European Space Agency's December 2022 figures. A recent paper in the journal Science calling for an international treaty to address space debris says there might be 100 trillion pieces of junk floating out there.

Some of these satellites have shattered due to accidental collision or deliberate destruction. A notable recent incident was a Russian anti-satellite debris test in 2021 that created so much debris it interfered with both ISS and Star link operations.

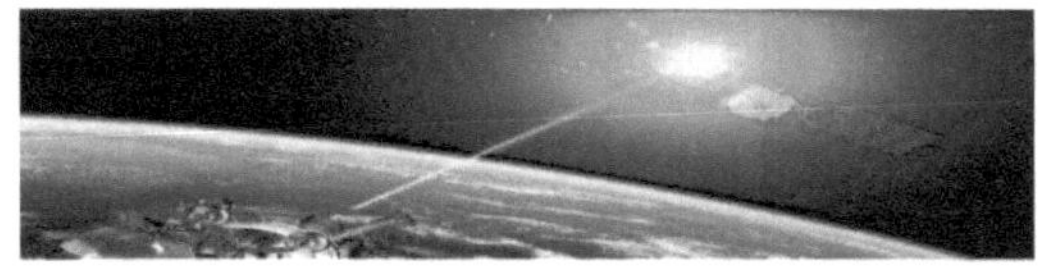

Remove Space Junk

10. NASA'S Space Cup Holes Drinks Without Gravity

NASA has been developing a space cup that can keep the liquid in its place even with an open top to make beverage consumption easier in space. Recently NASA showcased its futuristic anti-gravity space cup on Twitter.

A demo recently showcased NASA's futuristic space cup that can keep liquid collected even with an uncovered top, unlike sealed pouches that are currently used.

The new technology, works by taking advantage of the properties of fluid dynamics to mimic the effect of gravity, effectively keeping the liquid in place - even with an open lid. Astronaut Nicole Mann recently gave a demo in a video shared on Twitter wherein Mann puts coffee in the special cup, then gives it a spin to demonstrate how the liquid stays in place even as the cup flips over! It's quite remarkable that not even a single drop leaves the cup in the video. This special cup was designed as part of the Capillary Flow Experiment that is inspired by how surface tension exists on Earth while taking into account "wetting" conditions (what a liquid does in relation to a solid surface when brought together), and how the cup is built. Capillary action, or ways in which liquids ascend in solid shapes through forces of adhesion and cohesion, is actually the driving force of this magical cup. Owing to the capillary action between the beverage and the cup's wall, the drink sticks close to the rim instead of falling out even in an inverted state. According to a paper published in Nature Microgravity last year, a small amount of the beverage goes into the channel that runs from the bottom to the cup's rim, and the rest of the liquid stays at the bottom due to... you guessed it.... capillary action! The cup was invented with the help of astronaut Don Pettit who has also lived on the space station. Ref: NASA; India Times

Without Gravity

11.Shockwaves Recorded in Cosmic Web for First Time

If you could zoom out to look at the universe at its largest scale, you'd see that it's made up of a cosmic web. Now, web for the first time ever, providing new insights into cosmic-scale magnetic fields. When the universe was young, it was more or less uniform, with matter and magnetic fields essentially the same in all directions. But over time, the distribution of dark matter attracted matter to it, forming a gigantic network of dense filaments containing galaxies and clusters, threading between vast voids. This cosmic web was first theoretically proposed in the 1960s, and its structure was modeled in simulations beginning in the 1980s. More recently, astronomers have been able to map it out and observe the glow of its filaments. In the new study, scientists from the Centre for Radio Astronomy Research (ICRAR) have managed to observe radio emissions coming from shockwaves rolling through the cosmic web. Doing so wasn't easy, since the signals are extremely faint and hard to pick out of the background of all the other radio emissions blaring constantly through the universe.

So the team instead focused on a variation that's less common – polarized radio signals, which are produced in the cosmic web as the end result of a cascade of processes. Regions of the web that are denser with matter will attract even more matter through gravity. As matter falls into these regions it heats up the gases there, which radiate outwards as shockwaves. When these shockwaves reach the extremely cold voids, that interaction gives off polarized radio light.

The team used data from several projects and observatories, including the Global Magneto-Ionic Medium Survey, the Planck Legacy Archive, the Owens Valley Long Wavelength Array, and the Murchison Widefield Array. This allowed them to stack data of detected polarized radio emissions over the top of known cosmic web clusters and filaments, showing that the detections were indeed coming from the web. Ref: journal Science Advances

12. Largest Map Created with More Than 1 billion Galaxies

Astronomers released the largest 2-Dimensional map of the entire sky that took 6 years to create. By creating map of even the dimmest and most-properties of dark matter & dark energy.

The universe is teeming with galaxies, each brimming with billions of stars. Though all galaxies shine brightly, many are cloaked in dust, while others are so distant that to observers on Earth, they appear as little more than faint smudges. By creating comprehensive maps of even the dimmest and most-distant galaxies, astronomers are better able to study the structure of the universe and unravel the mysterious properties of dark matter and dark energy. The largest such map to date has just grown even larger, with the tenth data release from the DOE's Dark Energy Spectroscopic Instrument (DESI) Legacy Imaging Survey. The DESI Legacy Imaging Survey expands on the data included in two earlier companion surveys: the Dark Energy Camera (DEC am) Legacy Survey and the Beijing-Arizona Sky Survey. Jointly, these three surveys imaged 14,000 square degrees of the sky visible from the northern hemisphere, using telescopes at NSF's NOIR Lab's Kitt Peak National Observatory (KPNO) and Cerro Tolono Inter-American Observatory (CTIO) in Chile.

This ambitious six-year effort involved three telescopes, one petabyte of data, and 100 million CPU hours on one of the world's most powerful computers at the US Department of Energy's National Energy Research Scientific Computing Center. This effort culminated in the largest two-dimensional map of the sky ever created. One of the main purposes of this map is to identify roughly 40 million target galaxies for the DESI Spectroscopic Survey, which is aimed at understanding dark energy by precisely mapping the expansion history of the universe over the last 12 billion years. Ref: Forbes; NOIRLab

Galaxies

13.ISRO Plan for Venus Orbiter Mission

The Venus Orbiter Mission, also known as Shukrayaan-1, is an ambitious project by the Indian Space Research Organisation (ISRO) to explore Venus.

Objectives: -

Surface and Atmosphere Study: The mission aims to study the surface and atmosphere of Venus, focusing on its geological and atmospheric processes. Atmospheric Chemistry: It will investigate the atmospheric chemistry, dynamics, and compositional variations of Venus. Solar Interaction: The mission will also study the interaction between solar irradiance and the Venusian ionosphere.

Mission Details: -

Launch Date: Shukrayaan-1 is planned for launch in December 2024.

Spacecraft: The spacecraft will have a launch mass of approximately 2,500 kg and will carry a science payload of around 100 kg.

Orbit: The initial elliptical orbit around Venus is expected to be 500 km at periapsis and 60,000 km at apoapsis.

Instruments:

Synthetic Aperture Radar: This instrument will examine the Venusian surface, which is obscured by thick clouds, making it impossible to observe in visible light.

Venusian Neutrals Analyzer: A collaboration between Sweden and India, this instrument will study how charged particles from the sun interact with Venus's atmosphere.

Significance

First Mission to Venus: Shukrayaan-1 will be India's first mission to Venus, marking a significant milestone in ISRO's interplanetary exploration efforts.

Scientific Contributions: The mission is expected to provide valuable insights into Venus's extreme conditions, contributing to our understanding of planetary science and the evolution of terrestrial planets.

14.ISRO begins preparation for India's 2nd mission to Mars

India is readying to send another spacecraft to Mars, officials of the Indian Space Research Organisation have said, nine years after it created history by successfully placing a rocket on orbit around the red planet on its first attempt.

The Mars Orbiter Mission-2, informally known as Mangalyaan-2, would carry four payloads, according to documents accessed by HT. The scientific instruments will study aspects of Mars, including interplanetary dust, and the Martian atmosphere and environment. "All of these payloads are in different stages of development," an official said, declining to be named. Nine years ago on September 24, India created history by entering the orbit of Mars in its first attempt, a feat that had not been accomplished by any other space agency till then.

The RO experiment is being developed to measure neutral and electron density profiles. The instrument is essentially a microwave transmitter operating at X-band frequency that can help understand the behaviour of the Martian atmosphere. The objectives of the first mission were technological to showcase the design, realisation and launch of a Mars orbiter spacecraft capable of operating with sufficient autonomy during the journey to the red planet, to insert the craft into Mars orbit, and capture and complete the in-orbit phase around Mars. The first Mars mission carried five scientific payloads to study the planet's surface features, morphology, mineralogy and atmosphere.

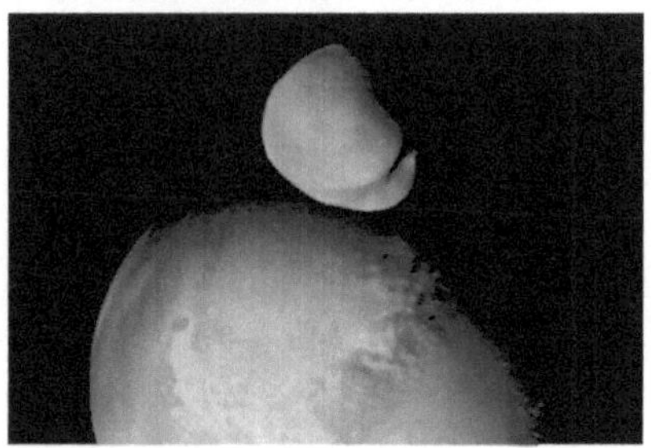

Mars

15.Scientists Found Forbidden Planet That Shouldn't Exist.

Astronomers discovers an unusual planetary system in which a large gas giant planet orbits a small red dwarf star called TOI-5205. As per our current understanding of planet formation, TO-5205b Should not exist; it is a "forbidden" planet.

Small stars are not expected to have gas giants around them. And yet astronomers found one.

Red dwarfs are the most common type of stars out there. They are smaller and less luminous than our Sun and live for much longer. They are also a great place for planets to form, but not every type of planet: current models suggest that they are an unlikely place for gas giants to form. So, imagine the surprise when astronomers found planet TOI-5205b. The planet is slightly larger and heavier than Jupiter but it orbits a star that is just a bit bigger. At 40 percent of the mass of the Sun, the ratio between the planet's mass versus the star's mass is 0.3 percent. The highest among all known planets orbiting red dwarfs. "The host star, TOI-5205, is just about four times the size of Jupiter, yet it has somehow managed to form a Jupiter-sized planet, which is quite surprising!" lead author Shubham Kanodia, from the Carnegie Institution for Science, said in a statement. Their findings challenge long-held ideas about planet formation. Ref: Carnegie Institution for Science; The Astronomical Journal

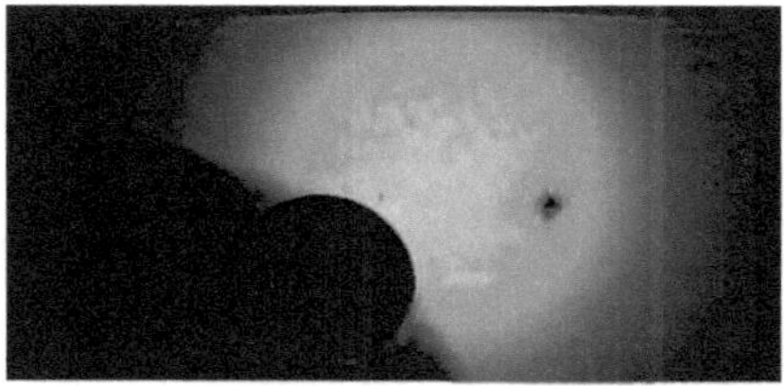

Forbidden Planet

16. Key Life -Forming Molecules Found in Asteroid Ryugu.

Analysis of samples brought back from the asteroid Ryugu show that this space rock contains some of the molecules needed for life that are in fact older than the solar system itself. This includes 15 amino acids, the building blocks of proteins. Asteroid Ryugu has a rich complement of organic molecules, according to a NASA and international team's initial analysis of a sample from the asteroid's surface delivered to Earth by Japan's Hayabusa2 spacecraft. The discovery adds support to the idea that organic material from space contributed to the inventory of chemical components necessary for life. Organic molecules are the building blocks of all known forms of terrestrial life and consist of a wide variety of compounds made of carbon combined with hydrogen, oxygen, nitrogen, sulfur, and other atoms. However, organic molecules can also be made by chemical reactions that don't involve life, supporting the hypothesis that chemical reactions in asteroids can make some of life's ingredients. The science of prebiotic chemistry attempts to discover the compounds and reactions that could have given rise to life, and among the prebiotic organics found in the sample were several kinds of amino acids. Certain amino acids are widely used by terrestrial life as a component to build proteins. Proteins are essential to life as they are used to make enzymes that speed up or regulate chemical reactions and to make structures from microscopic to large such as hair and muscles. The sample also contained many types of organics that form in the presence of liquid water, including aliphatic amines, carboxylic acids, polycyclic aromatic hydrocarbons, and nitrogen-containing heterocyclic compounds. "So far, the amino acid results from Ryugu are mostly consistent with what has been seen in certain types of carbon-rich (carbonaceous) meteorites that have been exposed to the most water in space," said Jason Dworkin of NASA's Goddard Space Flight Center in Greenbelt, Maryland, a co-author of the paper. Ref: NASA

Asteroid Ryugu

THREE

BIO TECHNOLOGY

1.Embryos Grew Abnormally Due to Nano plastics

In a new study, nano plastics have been found to interfere with stem cells, disrupting the early stages of development in chicken embryos, including severe heart defects. Nano plastics are a fraction smaller than micro plastics.

A new study of chicken embryos suggests that sufficient concentrations of teensy Nano plastics speckles could interfere with the earliest stages of development, glugging up stem cells from which tissues and organs usually emerge.

These tissue defects are far more serious and extensive than has been previously reported and include heart defects, which have not been described before in animal studies of micro plastics.

Under the focused gaze of fluorescent microscopes, biologist Meiru Wang of Leiden University in the

Netherlands injected samples of nanometer-scale glowing plastic particles across the embryonic gut wall and circulate into multiple organs of the chick embryos.

Nano plastics are a fraction smaller than micro plastics; both are typically produced when synthetic clothes shed plastic microfibers or larger plastics break down into ever smaller pieces under the glare of UV rays or mechanical weathering.

Past animal studies have tried to investigate the potential health risks of polystyrene micro plastics, finding biochemical signs of potentially toxic effects as they accumulate in the livers, kidneys, and guts of laboratory mice. While results like those only hint at what might be happening in humans, we have good reason to be concerned. Our dependency on cheaply made plastic goods and synthetic materials is polluting our oceans and air with microscopic shards of plastic polymers making their way into our bodies and out the other side. Studies have found micro plastics lodged deep in human lungs, circulating in our blood, and entering the placenta – the vital organ that shields unborn babies from pathogens and other potentially hazardous materials lurking in the mother's blood.

But the possible effects of micro plastics on the early development of cells and tissues that go on to form organs and bodies are largely unknown. Most studies of that kind have been in aquatic organisms, such as zebra fish.

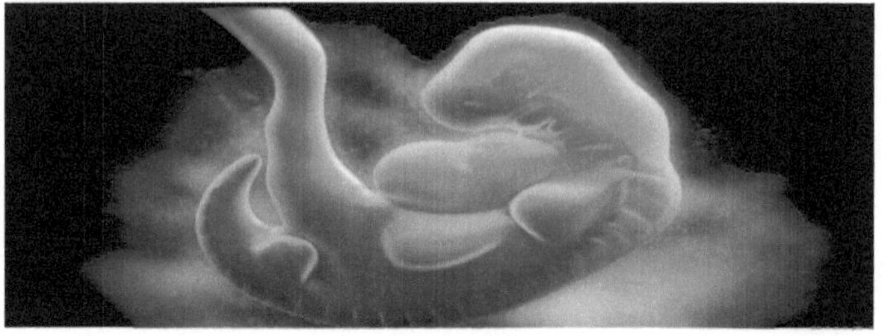

Chicken Embryos

2.New Technologies to control ageing

In a pioneering study, researchers from Harvard Medical School, University of Maine, and MIT have introduced a chemical method for reversing cellular aging. This revolutionary approach offers a potential alternative to gene therapy for age reversal. The findings could transform treatments for age-related diseases, enhance regenerative medicine, and potentially lead to whole-body rejuvenation. Groundbreaking Discovery in Aging Reversal In a monumental study, a team of researchers has revealed a novel approach to combating aging and age-related diseases. This work, undertaken by scientists at Harvard Medical School, introduces the first chemical method to rejuvenate cells, bringing them to a more youthful state. Prior to this, only powerful gene therapy could achieve this feat. On July 12, 2023, researchers from Harvard Medical School, the University of Maine, and the Massachusetts Institute of Technology (MIT) published a fresh research paper in Aging. The paper, titled, "Chemically induced reprogramming to reverse cellular aging," extends upon a previously groundbreaking discovery. The researchers are Jae-Hyun Yang, Christopher A. Petty, Thomas Dixon-McDougall, Maria Vina Lopez, Alexander Tyshkovskiy, Sun Maybury-Lewis, Xiao Tian, Nabilah Ibrahim, Zhili Chen, Patrick T. Griffin, Matthew Arnold, Jien Li, Oswaldo A. Martinez, Alexander Behn, Ryan Rogers-Hammond, Suzanne Angeli, Vadim N. Gladyshev, and David A. Sinclair.

Exploring the Methodology

This discovery builds on the finding that the expression of specific genes, known as Yamanaka factors, can transform adult cells into induced pluripotent stem cells (iPSCs). This breakthrough, which earned a Nobel Prize, prompted scientists to question if cellular aging could be reversed without pushing cells to become too young and potentially cancerous. In this recent study, the scientists probed for molecules that could, in tandem, revert cellular aging and refresh human cells. They designed advanced cell-based assays to differentiate between young and old, as well as senescent cells. The team employed transcription-based aging clocks and a real-time nucleocytoplasmic protein compartmentalization (NCC) assay. In a significant development, they identified six chemical combinations that could return NCC and genome-wide transcript profiles to youthful states, reversing transcriptomic age in less than a week.

Relevance and Potential Applications

The Harvard team has previously shown the possibility of reversing cellular aging without causing unregulated cell growth. This was done by inserting specific Yamanaka genes into cells using a viral vector. Studies on various tissues and organs like the optic nerve, brain, kidney, and muscle have yielded encouraging results, including improved vision and extended lifespan in mice.

Additionally, recent reports have documented improved vision in monkeys.

Lifespan almost doubled after genetic rewiring

By creating the gene oscillator, the scientists made the yeast cells continually switch between the two aging pathways, preventing them from committing to their pre-destined path of decline and death, slowing the cells' degeneration. Those yeast cells that were synthetically rewired and aged under the direction of the synthetic oscillator had an 82% increase in lifespan compared with control cells. And the genetic manipulation did not appear to adversely affect them, according to Prof. Hao, who told MNT: "The yeast cells survive nicely with a fast growth rate."

Implications on increasing healthy life years for people?

Prof. Hao suggested that there may be potential for this approach in people: "Both of the two regulators have counterparts in humans, so I do believe that the same strategy could be applied to human cells. In fact, that's our next step in the future." And Prof. Howard Salis, Principal Investigator at the Salis Lab, Penn State University, who was not involved in the study, agreed: "If the collective objective of these interventions is to maintain healthier cell states, then the risk and morbidity of age-associated diseases will be reduced." However, it is very early days, and although this study shows that it is possible to switch off aging mechanisms in a single-celled organism, there are many questions to be answered before the technology might be applied to people.

3.Success stories from Neuralink's trials

Neuralink has made significant progress in its clinical trials. Here are a couple of success stories:

Noland Arbaugh (First Participant):

Noland, paralyzed below the shoulders due to a diving accident, received the Neuralink implant. He demonstrated playing online chess with his mind, moving the cursor on his laptop using the Neuralink device. While the technology isn't perfect, it's a promising starting point for brain-computer interfaces (BCIs).

Alex (Second Participant):

Alex, the second participant in the PRIME Study, received the Neuralink implant.

His surgery went well, and he has been improving his abilities:

Within minutes, he controlled a cursor with his mind, surpassing previous BCI records.

He used CAD software (Fusion 360) to design a custom mount for his Neuralink charger. The goal is to enhance digital device control for people with quadriplegia

More about Neuralink's brain-computer interface.

Neuralink, founded by Elon Musk in 2016, is pioneering brain-computer interfaces (BCIs) that redefine human capabilities.

The Link (N1 Implant):

The N1 Implant is a fully implantable, cosmetically invisible brain-chip interface. It allows users to control computers or mobile devices wirelessly, anywhere they go Surgical robot inserts these fine threads precisely.

Biocompatible Enclosure: Hermetically sealed to withstand harsh physiological conditions.

Battery: Wirelessly charged for easy use.

Chips and Electronics: Custom, low-power chips process neural signals.

Threads: 1024 electrodes distributed across 64 ultra-thin threads record neural activity.

Seamless BCI Experience: -

Neuralink prioritizes ease of use for fast and reliable computer control. If you're interested in clinical trials, consider joining their Patient Registry

Noland Arbaugh

4. Scientist Can Generate New Neurons in The Brain

Biologists have discovered how to generate new neurons in the adult brain. This is an incredible breakthrough that can revolutionize research for neurodegenerative diseases such as Alzheimer's & Parkinson's and can lead to new treatments. A team of biologists has recently discovered how to awaken neural stem cells and reactivate them in adult mice. Some areas of the adult brain contain quiescent, or dormant, neural stem cells that can potentially be reactivated to form new neurons. However, the transition from quiescence to proliferation is still poorly understood. A team led by scientists from the Universities of Geneva (UNIGE) and Lausanne (UNIL) has discovered the importance of cell metabolism in this process and identified how to wake up these neural stem cells and reactivate them. Biologists succeeded in increasing the number of new neurons in the brain of adult and even elderly mice. Stem cells have the unique ability to continuously produce copies of themselves and give rise to differentiated cells with more specialized functions. Neural stem cells (NSCs) are responsible for building the brain during embryonic development, generating all the cells of the central nervous system, including neurons.

Surprisingly, NSCs persist in certain brain regions even after the brain is fully formed and can make new neurons throughout life. This biological phenomenon, called adult neurogenesis, is important for specific functions such as learning and memory processes.

However, in the adult brain, these stem cells become more silent or "dormant" and reduce their capacity for renewal and differentiation. As a result, neurogenesis decreases significantly with age. Researchers have uncovered a metabolic mechanism by which adult NSCs can emerge from their dormant state and become active. Ref: Journal Science Advance

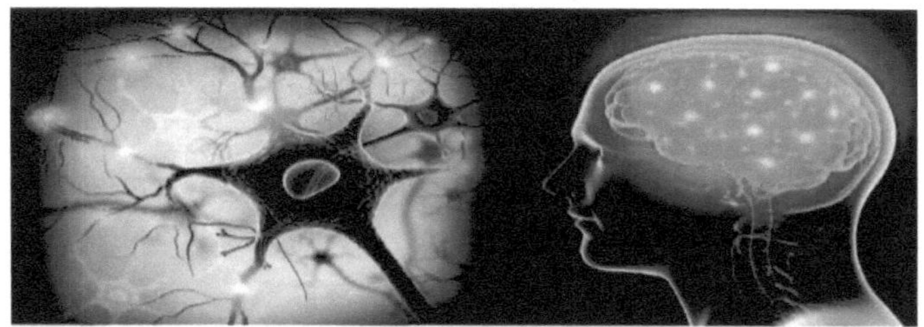

Human Brain

5.Scientists Solved Mystery Behind How We Smell?

Very little is known about how our olfactory receptors recognize specific odors and encode them differently in the brain. Now, for the first time, researcher have mapped the 3D structure of a human odor receptor, taking a step forward in understanding how we smell. Scientists from the University of California San Francisco (UCSF) have, for the first time, creating a precise, molecular-level, 3D structure of how an odor molecule activates an odorant receptor in humans.

The research focuses on an olfactory receptor, called OR51E2, and shows how it 'recognizes' the smell of cheese through certain molecular interactions that turn on the receptor. The odor receptors in our nose help us distinguish between the different kinds of smells-pleasant, pungent, and so on. But so far, little has been known about how these receptors detect molecules and convert them into scents. Now, with the first-ever 3D picture of the structure of our odor receptors, we might be closer than ever to solving the mystery behind how we smell. Odorant receptors—proteins present on the surface of olfactory cells that bind odor molecules—constitute half of the largest, most diverse type of receptors in humans. The human genome contains genes encoding 400 olfactory receptors.

In the 1920s, researchers predicted the human nose could differentiate about 10,000 smells, but a 2014 study suggests that we can distinguish over one trillion scents.

Each olfactory receptor can only interact with a specific set of odorants while a single odorant can activate multiple receptors. This can be compared to "hitting a chord on a piano", said Aashish Manglik, co-author of the study. "Instead of hitting a single note, it's a combination of keys that are hit that gives rise to the perception of a distinct odor." Ref: Nature Journal

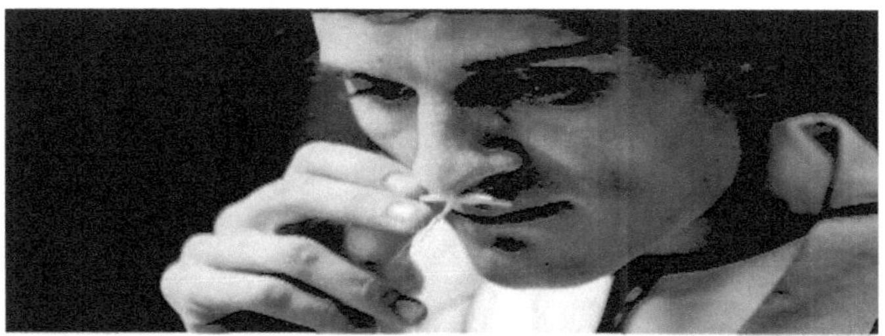

6.Bacteria Exhale Electricity as An Alternative to Oxygen.

Deep beneath the ocean floor, bacteria of the genus Geobacter send out protein nanowires, nearly 100,000 times thinner than a human hair to exhale electricity. These bacteria can be used to power small electronics.

These bizarre bacteria rely on two proteins, which band together in a single hair-like structure called a pilus. Many of these pili lie just beneath the bacterial membrane and help push the snorkels out of the cell and into the surrounding environment, thus allowing the microbe to breathe. This discovery not only reveals something unexpected about the bacteria's biology but could also pave the way for new technologies, from powerful microbe-powered batteries to new medical treatments for bacterial infections. The bacteria belong to the genus Geobacter and can be found all across the world, growing deep underground in soils that are totally devoid of oxygen. Humans rely on oxygen to convert food into usable energy and to sop up electrons that are left over from this metabolic process. If the leftover electrons accumulated, they would quickly become toxic to the body. Just like humans, Geobacter microbes generate waste electrons during metabolism, but they don't have access to oxygen like we do. So, to get rid of their excess electrons, the bacteria coat themselves in thin, conductive filaments, called nanowires, which can shuttle electrons out of the microbes and to other bacteria or minerals in the environment, such as iron oxide. These thin nanowires are 100,000 times smaller than the width of a human hair and can transport electrons over huge distances, hundreds to thousands of times the original microbe's body length.

Genus Geobacter

7.Scientists Discovered First Ever Virus-Eating Bacteria

*Scientists have discovered the **first-ever organism that eats viruses.** The unique organism is the first known **"Virovore"** or an organism that feeds on viruses. Scientists estimate each of* *these individual microbes can eat up to a **million viruses per day.***

Though we often think of viruses as being harmful, only a small percentage of the millions of known species are pathogens. In fact, viruses are all around us, playing helpful and intricate roles in our bodies and the environment.

Now, new research shows that they can also serve as food for certain microbes. In a study published in Proceedings of the National Academy of Sciences, researchers report that a small single-celled microbe, a ciliate in the genus Halteria, can subsist and grow entirely by consuming a certain type of virus. Scientists estimate each of these individual microbes can eat up to a million viruses per day, and in a small pond in their native habitat of North America, they could probably eat hundreds of trillions. Scientists knew that certain microbes can sometimes consume viruses, but it was thought to have minor importance nutritionally and otherwise, says John DeLong, study lead author and an evolutionary ecologist at the University of Nebraska–Lincoln. Viruses are packets of DNA or RNA that need host cells to reproduce, and which are thought to infect all living species. If microbes subsist on viruses, that significantly changes our understanding of how nutrients and elements like carbon move through the ecosystem. Ref: Proceedings of the National Academy of Sciences

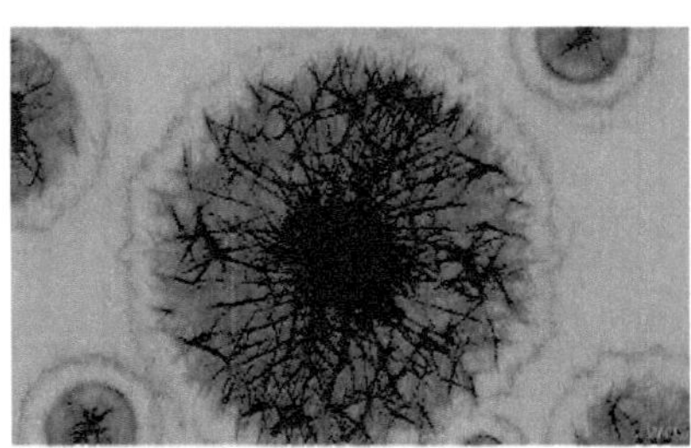

Virus-Eating Bacteria

8. The Eight-Year-old Android Developer with An IQ Of 180

*Meet **Rishi Shiv Prasanna**, the eight-year-old Android developer, who developed three apps for the Android app store. Prasanna has a **higher IQ than Albert Einstein**, who had an IQ of 160. By age 5, Prasanna had finished the entire Harry Potter.*

Indian President Droupadi Murmu felicitated 11 children with the Pradhan Mantri Rashtriya Bal Puraskar 2023. Among them was Rishi Shiv Prasanna, the eight-year-old boy genius from Bengaluru. Prassana won the award for developing three apps for the Android app store. With a verified IQ of 180, Prasanna's IQ is far higher than the average benchmark of 85-115 and much higher than the benchmark of 130 for highly intelligent individuals. Prasanna has a higher IQ than Albert Einstein, who had an IQ of 160. Prasanna is one of the youngest members of Mensa International, the oldest and most prestigious high-IQ society in the world. He joined the society at the age of 4 years and 5 months. But his feats aren't limited to just standardized tests of intelligence.

The little boy wonder learned to read at the age of two. By the age of three, when children are just starting to learn the alphabet, Prasanna could talk about the Solar System, the Universe, planets, shapes, and numbers. Prasanna mastered coding to the point where he became one of the youngest Google-certified Android developers. By age five, Prasanna had finished the entire Harry Potter series by JK Rowling. An impressive feat considering the seven books span over a million words in total. He has authored two books already.

9. 2-Million-Year-Old, World's Oldest DNA Discovered!

Scientists have made a significant breakthrough in reconstructing the history of our planet. **The oldest DNA** *ever recovered has revealed a remarkable 2-million-year-old* **ecosystem in Greenland**, *including the presence of an unlikely explorer:* **the mastodon.**

Sedimentary deposits from the permafrost of Greenland contained recoverable environmental DNA dating back to around 2 million years ago. That's 1 million years older than the previous record – DNA from a wooly mammoth that roamed the Siberian tundra 1 million years ago. This astonishing work has allowed a team of scientists to reconstruct an ancient landscape, revealing a world far removed from the icy shores of the Arctic Circle. "A new chapter spanning 1 million extra years of history has finally been opened, and for the first time, we can look directly at the DNA of a past ecosystem that far back in time," says geneticist Eske Willerslev of the University of Cambridge in the UK.

"DNA can degrade quickly, but we've shown that under the right circumstances, we can now go back further in time than anyone could have dared imagine."

Time is not kind to the remains of living things; DNA will rapidly degrade thanks to environmental stresses (such as hungry microbes), weather, and geological processes. If ancient DNA is to survive, it usually does so lock up in teeth and bones, where it is relatively protected. But material buried under the permafrost is also relatively protected.

Here, a range of samples collected from the ice and permafrost of the Kap København geologic formation in the mouth of a fjord in northern Greenland offered scientists the ability to recover and reconstruct environmental DNA from times long past.
Source: Science Alert; Nature Journal

10. Using Magnetic Bacteria to Plant Anti-Cancer Drug.

Scientists looking to harness the cancer-fighting capabilities of bacteria have made an impressive advance, demonstrating how magnetic forms of the microorganisms can be propelled into tumors.

The study was carried out at ETH Zurich in Switzerland and builds on previous work that demonstrated Magneto spirillum bacteria, which naturally contain iron oxide particles, can be controlled by magnetic fields. In 2020, the scientists used this technique to control the flow of liquids surrounding the bacteria in the laboratory, effectively turning them into magnetic micropumps. This raised the possibility of using them to deliver drugs in the body, by steering them to the desired location in the bloodstream. But exiting the bloodstream and entering tumor tissue isn't like hopping off of a train. The walls of blood vessels are densely packed barriers made up of cells, and only by squeezing through the narrow but fluctuating spaces in between those cells can certain molecules make it through. The scientists injected Magneto spirillum bacteria into mice and with a rotating magnetic field, showed that they could bolster their ability to sneak through these temporary gaps in the vessel walls. This enabled them to enter the tumor and from there, the bacteria were able to travel into the tumor of their own accord. "We make use of the bacteria's natural and autonomous locomotion as well," said Simone Schürle, who led the study. "Once the bacteria have passed through the blood vessel wall and are in the tumor, they can independently migrate deep into its interior."

11. Bees Have 8X Higher Electric Charge Than Thunderstorm

Researchers have found that insects can produce as much electric charge in the atmosphere as a thunderstorm cloud by observing the electrical fields around swarming honeybees. This kind of energy aids in influencing weather patterns.

By measuring the electrical fields near swarming honeybees, researchers have discovered that insects can produce as much atmospheric electric charge as a thunderstorm cloud. This type of electricity helps shape weather events, aids insects in finding food, and lifts spiders up in the air to migrate over large distances.

The research, published on October 24 in the journal I Science, demonstrates that living things can have an impact on atmospheric electricity. "We always looked at how physics influenced biology, but at some point, we realized that biology might also be influencing physics," says first author Ellard Hunting, a biologist at the University of Bristol. "We're interested in how different organisms use the static electric fields that are virtually everywhere in the environment." As with most living creatures, bees carry an innate electric charge. Having found that honeybee hive swarms change the atmospheric electricity by 100 to 1,000 volts per meter, increasing the electric field force normally experienced at ground level, the team developed a model that can predict the influence of other species of insects. "We only recently discovered that biology and static electric fields are intimately linked and that there are many unsuspected links that can exist over different spatial scales, ranging from microbes in the soil and plant-pollinator interactions to insect swarms and perhaps the global electric circuit," says Ellard.

12. Scientists Found an Animal That Can "Regrow" Its brain!

Scientists from **Switzerland and Austria** *That Axolotls (Ambystoma mexicanum), Known for their ability to regenerate their spinal cord, heart, and limbs, aquatic salamanders can also partially* **regenerate their brains** *if part of it is removed.*

The scientists wanted to test whether axolotls can regenerate all types of cells in their brains, including the connections that link one part of this organ to another. To do this, they created an atlas of the cells that make up the brains of these creatures. Different types of cells have different functions. They can play different roles because they express different genes. Understanding what types of cells are present in the brain and what they do allows us to understand the big picture of how it works. It also allows you to draw evolutionary parallels and look for common trends across species. The researchers performed RNA sequencing to identify the various cells that make up the axolotl's brain, including different types of neurons and progenitor cells.

They determined which genes are active when progenitor

cells become neurons. It turned out that many of them pass through an intermediate type called neuroblasts. Using RNA sequencing, scientists were able to capture all new cells during their regeneration in the period from one to 12 weeks after damage. The researchers found that all types of cells that were removed were eventually restored. An animal's brain regenerates in three stages. The first phase begins with a rapid increase in progenitor cells, and a small proportion of these cells activate the wound healing process. In the second phase, progenitor cells begin to differentiate into neuroblasts. Finally, in the third phase, neuroblasts differentiate into the same types of neurons that were originally lost. The most surprising thing for scientists was that the lost connections between the remote area of the brain and its other lobes were also restored. This indicates that the regenerated area also restored its functions.

13. Scientists Have Created RC Cyborg Cockroaches!

*Japanese scientists have engineered **remote-controlled cyborg cockroaches**. These Cyborg cockroaches are equipped with a tiny wireless control module powered by a **rechargeable battery** attached to a solar cell.*

Researchers have engineered a system for creating remote-controlled cyborg cockroaches, equipped with a tiny wireless control module that is powered by a rechargeable battery attached to a solar cell. Despite the mechanical devices, ultrathin electronics and flexible materials allow the insects to move freely. These achievements will help make the use of cyborg insects a practical reality. An international team led by researchers at the RIKEN Cluster for Pioneering Research (CPR) reported the results today (September 5, 2022) in the scientific journal *npj Flexible Electronics*. Scientists have been trying to design cyborg insects—part insect, part machine—to help inspect hazardous areas and monitor the environment. For the use of cyborg insects to be practical, however, handlers must be able to control them remotely for long stretches of time. This entails wireless control of their leg segments, powered by a tiny rechargeable battery.

Keeping the battery adequately charged is critical—nobody wants a suddenly out-of-control swarm of cyborg cockroaches roaming around. While docking stations for recharging the battery could be built, the need to return and recharge could disrupt time-sensitive missions. Therefore, an optimum approach is to include an onboard solar cell that can continuously ensure that the battery stays charged.

Of course, all of this is easier said than done. To successfully integrate these devices into a cockroach that has limited surface area required the engineering team to develop a special backpack and ultrathin organic solar cell modules. They also needed an adhesion system that keeps the machinery attached for long periods of time while still allowing natural movements.

Led by Kenjiro Fukuda, RIKEN CPR, the research team experimented with Madagascar cockroaches, which are approximately 6 cm (2.4 inches) long. They attached the wireless leg-control module and lithium polymer battery to the top of the insect on the thorax using a specially designed backpack. This was modeled after the body of a model cockroach and 3D printed with an elastic polymer. The result was a backpack that conformed perfectly to the curved surface of the cockroach, allowing the rigid electronic device to be stably mounted on the thorax for more than a month.

The ultrathin 0.004 mm thick organic solar cell module was mounted on the back side of the abdomen. "The body-mounted ultrathin organic solar cell module achieves a power output of 17.2 mW, which is more than 50 times larger than the power output of current state-of-the-art energy harvesting devices on living insects," according to Fukuda.

The ultrathin and flexible organic solar cell, and how it was attached to the insect, proved necessary to ensure freedom of movement. After carefully examining natural cockroach movements, the scientists realized that the abdomen changes shape and portions of the exoskeleton overlap. To accommodate this, they interleaved adhesive and non-adhesive sections onto the films, which allowed them to bend but also stay attached. When thicker solar cell films were tested, or when the films were uniformly attached, the cockroaches took twice as long to run the same distance. They also had difficulty righting themselves when on their backs. Once these components were integrated into the cockroaches, along with wires that stimulate the leg segments, the new cyborgs were tested. The battery was charged with pseudo-sunlight for 30 minutes, and animals were made to turn left and right using the wireless remote control. "Considering the deformation of the thorax and abdomen during basic locomotion, a hybrid electronic system of rigid and flexible elements in the thorax and ultrasoft devices in the abdomen appears to be an effective design for cyborg cockroaches," says Fukuda. "Moreover, since abdominal deformation is not unique to cockroaches, our strategy can be adapted to other insects like beetles, or perhaps even flying insects like cicadas in the future."

14. How Many Bacteria Is on Earth? 5 Nonillion!

*There are **five nonillion bacteria** in our ecosystem, including the ones found in living being. That is five with **30 zeros** after it! If we stack all the bacteria on top of each other, they would create a line that would be a **trillion light years** away from Earth.*

Bacteria are when it comes to straight numbers, the biggest population of organisms that exist on Earth. Bacteria can be found almost anywhere on the planet, deep underground, below the deepest points in the oceans, and even 50km high up in the atmosphere.

The estimated number of bacteria that exist within the Earth's system might shock you. You should also grab a bigger piece of paper if you want to write this down.

The total estimate of bacteria that live around us is five million trillion trillion. Sounds like a bunch of trillions, but the number would look like this: 5,000,000,000,000,000,000,000,000,000,000. An easier way of putting this would be "five with 30 zeros after it" or, if you are a strict mathematician: 5×10 to the 30th power. Somebody calculated, taking the average size of bacteria into account how much distance would all the bacteria stacked on top of each other. As it turns out, that long chain of bacteria would extend for a trillion light-years. This sounds almost scary, more so because of the fact that we are talking about microscopic-sized organisms. Something we can not even see with the naked eye is absolutely everywhere and in absolutely everyone. In today's day and age, when the world is still unable to handle the coronavirus pandemic, we have witnessed how the perspectives on hygiene and public health have massively changed. You might think that bacteria, especially when you think of that "5 with 30 zeros after it" number, are bad for other living things. Yes, bacteria can cause various diseases and infections, but out of all the bacteria that exist around us, less than one percent would, technically speaking, be considered dangerous.

15. Sharks Are Now 'Walking' On Land to Survive!

Climate change is making sharks walk on land. The epaulette shark, a species of long tailed carpet sharks, is evolving and now can walk on land for up to 2 hours to escape warming oceans. The shark has recently been found to move 98 feet on land.

We have all heard and seen sharks that swim in the ocean. But nature is here to surprise us. Scientists have recently found a shark species that can actually walk on land. Well, interesting! Scientists at Florida Atlantic University found that young epaulette sharks are capable of walking with their fins. Additionally, these sea creatures can also stay without oxygen for around 2 hours. The researchers stated that these features were developed in these sharks in response to the challenging environmental conditions. As per researchers, young epaulette sharks are found in southern Australia's Great Barrier Reef where they can be isolated due to the outgoing tide. In such situations, the sharks use their paddle-shaped fins to move "into small reef crevices" to protect themselves from "aerial and aquatic predators". Scientists are now looking into how these changes affect the shark's early development. Meanwhile, other walking shark species can be found in Australia, Indonesia, and Papua New Guinea.

16. World's First Synthetic Embryo Without Eggs or Sperms!

*Researchers have created the world's first ever lab-grown **"synthetic embryos"** which bypass the need for sperms, eggs, uterus, and even fertilization. To achieve this feat, researchers **used only stem cells and a spinning device.***

For the first time, scientists have created mouse embryos in the lab without using any eggs or sperm and watched them grow outside the womb. To achieve this feat, the researchers used only stem cells and a spinning device filled with shiny glass vials.

This is an important landmark in our understanding of how embryos build themselves. The breakthrough experiment took place in a specially designed bioreactor that serves as an artificial womb for developing embryos. Within the device, embryos float in small beakers of nutrient-filled solution, and the beakers are all locked into a spinning cylinder that keeps them in constant motion. This movement simulates how blood and nutrients flow to the placenta. The device also replicates the atmospheric pressure of a mouse uterus.

In addition to serving as a research model, the artificial womb could also someday serve as an incubator for cells, tissues and organs grown for transplant procedures.

17. Could Apple's next AirPods analyze your brain signals?

There have long been rumors about Apple adding health sensors to a future version of AirPods, including mechanisms that could detect noise levels and body temperature, according to well-connected *Bloomberg* reporter Mark Gurman. However, other companies are exploring in-ear wearables that set their sights on the last frontier of health and wellness technology: the brain. Companies like Elon Musk's Neuralink are looking into hardware that's actually implanted into your brain, but other firms are researching much less invasive options that could, theoretically, fit into a pair of Apple AirPods.

The result could be a brain-computer interface that lets users continuously monitor their brain for health and well-being purposes. Here's what you should know.

A wearable that monitors brain signals

In March, a lesser-known wearables manufacturer called Aware Custom Biometric Wearables announced a new study that validated one of its flagship products — something called the Ear-EEG.

The Ear-EEG is a novel device that fits into your ears like AirPods or other headphones. Instead of playing music, however, the device is meant to monitor brain activity through ambulatory recording. Technically, it performs an EEG, or electroencephalogram, which measures brain activity through electrical signals. According to Aware, the wearable fits deep into the ear canal. This positioning places custom electrodes and sensors near the brain, the auricular branch of the vagus nerve, and major blood vessels.

The result is high-quality EEG data, real-time brain analysis, and vagus nerve stimulation. "Aware captures an unprecedented amount of brain data, delivering personalized, AI-driven health and human performance insights into the body and brain in a device you wear in your daily life," CEO Sam Kellett Jr. said in a press release.

As far as what the study found, it validated Aware's claims that Ear-EEG could capture medical-grade EEG data. With machine learning, the system was also able to detect seizures in epilepsy patients. Taking a broader view, the company says it's excited because of "the ear's unique capabilities." Combining continuous biometric monitoring with AI analytics means deeper insights into our neurological health. "Aware's method unlocks potential across a wide range of medical applications, enhancing our understanding of neurological health and refining disease management strategies," said Rob Matthews, CTO of Aware.

Google's brain signal device

It isn't just smaller companies that are exploring using wearables to read brain waves. Google off-shoot NextSense is also researching earbuds that can read the brain's electrical signals.

More specifically, NextSense is experimenting with a device that fits into the ear canal and performs an EEG, much like Aware's Ear-EEG. Like Aware's focus on seizure detection in its study, Google's subsidiary is looking at sleep and neurological conditions, *Wired* reported.

Also, like Aware, the team found that their wearables were surprisingly accurate at detecting oncoming seizures. Despite the success, there are reasons to believe that this technology isn't ready for prime time yet. For example, one of the researchers described EEGs as one of "the worst sensors in the world." Because of factors like body motion, environmental noise, and surface noise, EEG sensors can have a hard time parsing out useful data. More than that, packing the kind of sensors required for an EEG into an in-ear wearable is no small feat.

However, like Aware, the researchers at NextSense were pleasantly surprised by the accuracy of their results. "I thought, OK, it shouldn't work," John Stivoric, one of the researchers, told *Wired*. "But it does work. These signals are showing up. How is this even possible?" Based on the team's research, NextSense submitted them

Could AirPods read brain signals?

Theoretically, AirPods could perform a similar EEG function to the two other wearables described in this article. Although both wearables are clunkier and larger than AirPods, it's only a matter of time before the sensors can be shrunk down to a manageable size.

Of course, AirPods that can read the electrical activity in your brain are likely years away, but there's reason to believe that this type of health tech is on Apple's radar. Apple has been exploring the brain and related technology. For example, back in 2022, Apple began hiring researchers that specialized in neuroscience and engineering, including computational neuroscientists.

If all that wasn't clear enough, Apple in 2023 filed a patent application for an AirPods-like device that was specifically equipped with an EEG.

This patent application becomes even more interesting when Apple's researchers describe how the same type of sensor suite could be embedded in a pair of smart glasses.

So, Apple may not only be working on AirPods that monitor brain signals, but Apple Vision Pro or similar wearables and smart glasses with the same capabilities.

What could these AirPods help with?

As far as *why* you'd want your AirPods to monitor your brain signals, there are a wide range of use cases. Both Aware and NextSense found that their devices were useful in detecting oncoming seizures, for example.

There are other use cases, however, such as:

- Biometric identification
- Long-term sleep monitoring
- Driver drowsiness detection
- Detection of diseases, such as inflammation or tumors.

And, of course, there's some promising research suggesting that in-ear EEG sensors could be used to create a brain-computer interface. This type of application could, in theory, allow you to control a device with nothing but your thoughts. Or, more accurately, the electrical signals that your thoughts create. Compared to actual implantable chips, this could be much less invasive, and likely much more affordable to a more general population.

In other words, Apple may not just be researching AirPods that read brain signals, but AirPods that use your brain signals to control your other devices.

FOUR
SCIENTIFIC RESEARCH

1. Scientists Finally Detected Neutrino in Particle Collider

For the very first time, physicists have detected high-energy neutrinos aka ghost particle inside the world's largest atom smasher Large Hadron Collider. The findings could help unlock the secrets of how stars go supernova.

The tiny particles, known as neutrinos, were spotted by the FASER neutrino detector at the Large Hadron Collider (LHC) — the world's largest particle accelerator.

Neutrinos earn their spectral nickname because their non-existent electrical charge and almost zero mass mean they barely interact with other types of matter. True to their ghostly moniker, neutrinos fly through regular matter at close to the speed of light.

"We've discovered neutrinos from a brand-new source — particle colliders — where you have two beams of particles smash together at extremely high energy," Jonathan Feng, a physicist at the University of California Irvine and a co-spokesperson of the FASER Collaboration, said in a statement. Every second, about 100 billion neutrinos pass through each square centimeter of your body. The tiny particles are everywhere — produced in the nuclear fire of stars, in enormous supernova explosions, by cosmic rays and radioactive decay, and in particle accelerators and nuclear reactors on Earth. In fact, neutrinos, which were first discovered zipping out from a nuclear reactor in 1956, are second only to photons as the most abundant subatomic particles in the universe. But despite their ubiquity, the chargeless and nearly massless particles' minimal interactions with other matter make them incredibly difficult to detect. Despite this many famous neutrino detection experiments — such as Japan's Super-Kamiokande detector, Fermilab's Mini Boone, and the Antarctic Ice Cube detector — have been able to spot solar-generated neutrinos. But the neutrinos arriving to us from the sun are just one small slice of the ghost particles out there. On the other end of the energy spectrum are the high-energy neutrinos produced in gigantic supernova explosions and in particle showers when deep-space particles slam into Earth's atmosphere. These high-energy ghosts have remained a mystery to scientists until now.

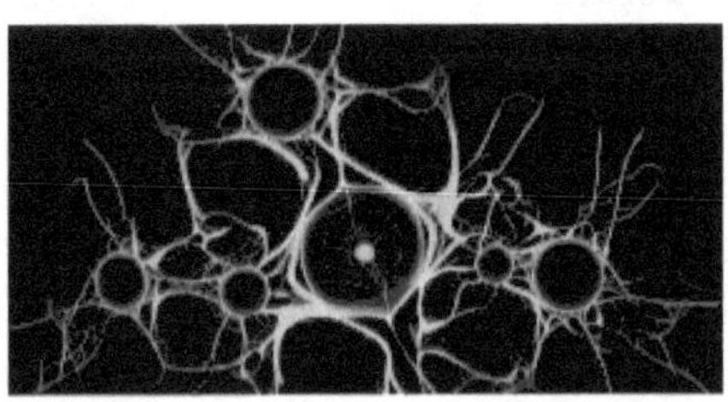

Detected Neutrino

2.COVID or Flu? Checking Device.

A sensor created by scientists at the University of Texas can screen for both the flu and COVID at the same time and can identify which one you have in less than ten second. It can detect & differentiate between the presence of various viral proteins.

Have a cough, sore throat, and congestion? Any number of respiratory viruses could be responsible. Conventional tests can identify certain likely culprits by relying on chemical reactions, but some researchers want to swap chemistry for electrical changes sensed by nanomaterials. Recently, scientists report using a single-atom-thick nonmaterial to build a device that can simultaneously detect the presence of the viruses that cause COVID-19 and the flu — at much lower levels and much more quickly than conventional tests for either.

The researchers presented their results at the spring meeting of the American Chemical Society (ACS). The symptoms of both flu and COVID-19 overlap considerably, making it difficult to distinguish between them, notes Deji Akinwande, Ph.D., who presented the work at the meeting. "When both of these viruses are circulating together as they did earlier this winter, it would be immensely useful to have a sensor that can simultaneously detect whether you have COVID, flu, none of the above, or both," he said. Akinwande, who is at The University of Texas at Austin, said that the device he and colleagues are developing could be modified to test for other infections as well. The group, including Dmitry Kireev, Ph.D., a post doc in Akinwande's lab, constructed the COVID-19 and flu sensor using grapheme, a single layer of carbon atoms arranged in a hexagonal lattice pattern.

Its extreme thinness renders grapheme highly sensitive to any electrical changes in its environment. Akinwande and other researchers see enormous potential in using it and other, similar nanomaterials to create sensors for many different applications. "These ultra-thin nanomaterials generally hold the record for best sensitivity, even down to the detection of single atoms, and they can improve the ability to detect very small quantities of basically anything that needs to be sensed, whether it's bacteria or viruses, in gas or blood," Akinwande said. Ref: American Chemical Society (ACS)

How to Use the Test:

Follow the instructions provided with the test kit carefully. Generally, you will need to swab the inside of your nostrils, place the swab in a vial with a solution, and then insert the vial into the test device. After a specified amount of time (usually around 15-30 minutes), the device will display the results.

Checking Device

3.Scientists Built a Mirror That 'Reflects Time Backwards

Scientists from the City University of New York have reflected an electromagnetic wave backward in time, for the first time ever. This discovery could lead to new, unusual ways to control light, such as photonic time crystals. Light can reflect off mirrors, and sounds off surfaces. However, scientists have long theorized about time reflections, where a signal passing through a time "interface" would act like it was traveling backward in time. Now a new study for the first time demonstrates time reflections with light waves.

In a paper published in Nature Physics, a team from the City University of New York has reflected part of an electromagnetic wave backward in time.

It's the first time this mind-bending feat has been achieved with this particular type of signal, and their technique could eventually help engineers create computers that send super-fast signals through light.

The kind of light or sound reflections that we're used to, also known as spatial reflections, happens when a wave meets a roadblock of sorts—some physical surface that it can't pass through. Instead of continuing on its merry way, the wave bounces back.

"Light bounces off a mirror because the impedance of the mirror material is very different to air, so the waves that hit the mirror have to go back, they can't enter the mirror," study co-author Andrea Alù told Motherboard.

Time reflection is similar, said Alù, except that instead of a physical roadblock, a time mirror works by creating an abrupt change in time. "The larger the contrast, the stronger the time reflection will be," he said. In their study, Alù and his team built a time "mirror" by creating a material capable of literally bending space and time—a so-called metamaterial. The material looks like a large plastic board covered in a long strip of metal weaving back and forth.

The metal is loaded with a dense collection of switches that can be flipped on and off faster than the frequency of the incoming wave. This abrupt switching is what creates the mirror. Ref: Journal Nature Physics.

Mirror

4.Mount Everest Has Frozen Germs for Centuries

Scientists have found out Mount Everest is freezing microbes coming out of your sneeze and cough. According to the research, humans are leaving behind a frozen legacy of microbes, which can lie dormant for decades or even centuries.

A new study has found out Mount Everest is freezing microbes coming out of your sneeze and cough. According to the new University of Colorado Boulder-led research, climbers, and travelers are leaving behind a frozen legacy of hardy microbes, which can withstand harsh conditions at high elevations and lie dormant in the soil for decades or even centuries. "There is a human signature frozen in the microbiome of Everest, even at that elevation," said Steve Schmidt, senior author of the paper and professor of ecology and evolutionary biology. Schmidt added, "If somebody even blew their nose or coughed, that's the kind of thing that might show up. "The team also found that the microbes seemed to have evolved. The soil samples were collected by researchers who went to Everest in 2019 to set up the planet's highest weather station.

Mount Everest

5.Scientists Can Now Turn Air into Electricity

Australian researchers have uncovered a special enzyme named Huc capable of transforming air into energy. This breakthrough paves the way for the development of devices that can literally generate energy from thin air.

Australian researchers have uncovered an enzyme capable of transforming air into energy. The study, which was recently published in the prestigious journal Nature, shows that the enzyme utilizes small amounts of hydrogen in the air to generate an electrical current. The discovery was made by a team of scientists led by Dr. Rhys Grinter, Ashleigh Kropp, a Ph.D. student, and Professor Chris Greening from the Monash University Biomedicine

Discovery Institute in Melbourne, Australia. The team produced and studied a hydrogen-consuming enzyme sourced from a bacterium commonly found in soil.

Recent work by the team has shown that many bacteria use hydrogen from the atmosphere as an energy source in nutrient-poor environments. "We've known for some time that bacteria can use the trace hydrogen in the air as a source of energy to help them grow and survive, including in Antarctic soils, volcanic craters, and the deep ocean," Professor Greening said. "But we didn't know how they did this, until now."

In this Nature paper, the researchers extracted the enzyme responsible for using atmospheric hydrogen from a bacterium called Mycobacterium smegmatis. They showed that this enzyme, called Huc, turns hydrogen gas into an electrical current.

Dr. Grinter notes, "Huc is extraordinarily efficient. Unlike all other known enzymes and chemical catalysts, it even consumes hydrogen below atmospheric levels – as little as 0.00005% of the air we breathe." Huc is a "natural battery" that produces a sustained electrical current from the air or added hydrogen. While this research is at an early stage, the discovery of Huc has considerable potential to develop small air-powered devices, for example as an alternative to solar-powered devices. Ref: Nature Journal.

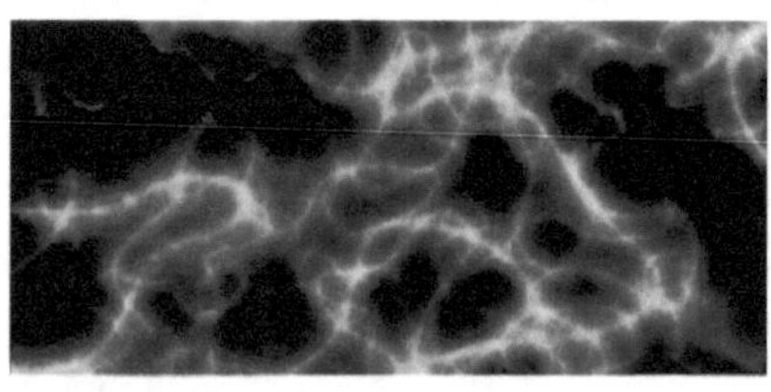

Air into Electricity

6. This Camera Shoots at A Trillionth of a Second!

Researchers have developed a new kind of camera with a shutter speed equipment to one picosecond. Speeding up a shutter a million million times will enable researchers to see atom frozen in time, the same way that we freeze motion as photos. To take a picture, the best digital cameras on the market open their shutter for around four-thousandths of a second. To snapshot atomic activity, you'd need a shutter that clicks a lot faster. Now scientists have come up with a way of achieving a shutter speed that's a mere trillionth of a second, or 250 million times faster than those digital cameras. That makes it capable of capturing something very important in materials science: dynamic disorder.

Simply put, it's when clusters of atoms move and dance around in a material in specific ways over a certain period – triggered by a vibration or a temperature change, for example. It's not a phenomenon that we fully understand yet, but it's crucial to the properties and reactions of materials. The new super-speedy shutter speed system gives us much more insight into what's happening with the dynamic disorder. The researchers are referring to their invention as variable shutter atomic pair distribution function or vs PDF for short. "It's only with this new vs PDF tool that we can really see this side of materials," says materials scientist Simon Billing from Columbia University in New York.

"With this technique, we'll be able to watch a material and see which atoms are in the dance and which are sitting it out." Ref: Journal Nature Materials, Science Alert

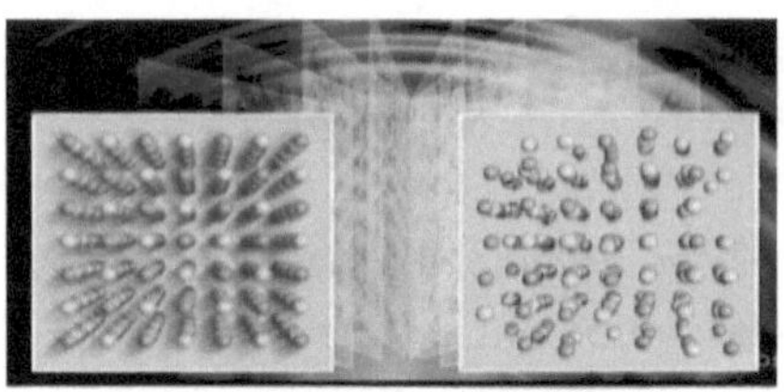

Camera Shoots

7.Scientist querious about Mission-Gaganyaan?

Gaganyaan pronunciation from Sanskrit: gagana, "celestial" and yāna, "craft, vehicle") is an Indian crewed orbital spacecraft intended to be the formative spacecraft of the Indian Human Spaceflight Programme. The spacecraft is being designed to carry three people, and a planned upgraded version will be equipped with rendezvous and docking capabilities. In its maiden crewed mission, the Indian Space Research Organisation (ISRO)'s largely autonomous 5.3-metric ton capsule will orbit the Earth at 400 km altitude for up to seven days with a two- or three-person crew on board. The first crewed mission was originally planned to be launched on ISRO's HLVM3 rocket in December 2021. As of October 2023, it is expected to be launched by 2025. The Hindustan Aeronautics Limited (HAL)-manufactured crew module underwent its first uncrewed experimental flight on December 18, 2014. As of May 2019, design of the crew module has been completed. Defence Research and Development Organisation (DRDO) will provide support for critical human-centric systems and technologies such as space-grade food, crew healthcare, radiation measurement and protection, parachutes for the safe recovery of the crew module, and the fire suppression system. On June 11, 2020, it was announced that the first uncrewed Gaganyaan launch would be delayed due to the COVID-19 pandemic in India. The overall timeline for crewed launches was expected to remain unaffected. ISRO chairman S. Somanath announced in 2022 that the first crewed mission would not take place until 2024 at the earliest because of safety concerns.

The Gaganyaan Mission will be led by V. R. Lalithambika, the former Director of the Directorate of the Human Spaceflight Programme with ISRO Chairman S Somnath and S. Unnikrishnan Nair, Director of Vikram Sarabhai Space Centre. Imtiaz Ali Khan superseded V. R. Lalithambika as the Director of the Directorate of Human Spaceflight Programme.

Objectives of Gaganyaan Mission

The Gaganyaan Mission is an ambitious and co-ordinated project of ISRO in collaboration with other agencies, such as various research labs, Indian academia, and industries, with the following objectives:

To undertake human space flights: Its immediate aim is to demonstrate indigenous capability to undertake human space flights.

Space exploration: In the long run, it will lay the foundation for a sustained Indian human space exploration programme.

Technologies Required for ISRO's Gaganyaan Mission

In order to ensure crew safety in this programme, various precautionary and safety measures were required. In this regard, ISRO required major new technologies for the

Gaganyaan Mission such as Human rated launch vehicle, a habitable orbital module, crew escape systems, and a life support system.

Gaganyaan Mission

8. Scientists Found an Entirely New Way of Measuring Time.

The new experiments on the wave-like nature of something called a Rydberg state assure that the measured time is correct. Unlike any other clock, this quantum watch does not utilize a counter and is fully quantum mechanical in its nature.

Determining the passage of time in our world of ticking clocks and oscillating pendulums is a simple case of counting the seconds between 'then' and 'now'.

Down at the quantum scale of buzzing electrons, however, 'then' can't always be anticipated. Worse still, 'now' often blurs into a haze of vagueness.

A potential solution could be found in the very shape of the quantum fog itself, according to a 2022 study by researchers from Uppsala University in Sweden.

Their experiments on the wave-like nature of something

called a Rydberg state revealed a novel way to measure time that doesn't require a precise starting point. Rydberg atoms are the over-inflated balloons of the particle kingdom. Puffed up with lasers instead of air, these atoms contain electrons in extremely high energy states, orbiting far from the nucleus.

Of course, not every pump of a laser needs to puff an atom up to cartoonish proportions. In fact, lasers are routinely used to tickle electrons into higher energy states for a variety of uses. In some applications, a second laser can be used to monitor the changes in the electron's position, including the passing of time. These 'pump-probe' techniques can be used to measure the speed of certain ultrafast electronics, for instance.

The mathematical rule book behind this wild game of Rydberg electron roulette is referred to as a Rydberg wave packet. Just like actual waves, having more than one Rydberg wave packet rippling about in a space creates interference, resulting in unique patterns of ripples. Throw enough Rydberg wave packets into the same atomic pond, and those unique patterns will each represent the distinct time it takes for the wave packets to evolve in accordance with one another.

It was these very 'fingerprints' of time that the physicists behind this set of experiments set out to test, showing they were consistent and reliable enough to serve as a form of quantum timestamping. Ref: New Scientist; Physical Review Research

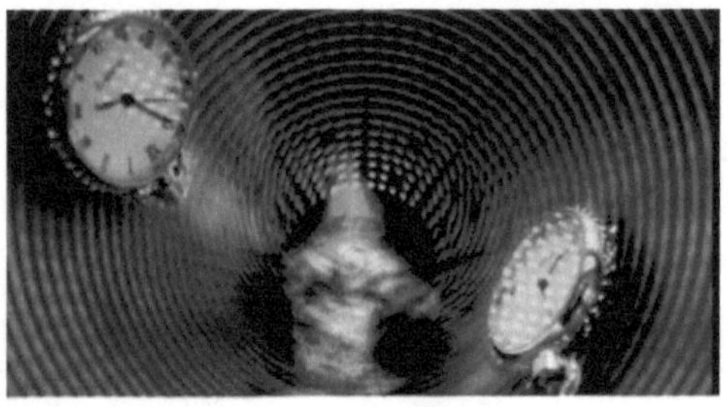

Time Machine

9. Now Scientists Can Reverse Time in A Quantum System.

Scientists have discovered a way to speed up, slow down, and even reverse quantum time by taking advantage of unusual properties within a quantum world in specific ways. "We have made science friction come true!" the researchers exclaimed. An Austrian and Spanish team demonstrated that a process can be 'rewound' to restore the components of an atom to their previous state.

Imagine you are 40-something and want to go on a date looking like you did 20 years ago. This is impossible in the classical physical world but not in the quantum world, which refers to the subatomic particles that are the foundation for all reality. In a series of six papers, the team from the Austrian Academy of Sciences and the University of Vienna detailed their findings. The familiar laws of physics don't map intuitively onto the subatomic world, which is made up of quantum particles called qubits that can technically exist in more than one state simultaneously, a phenomenon known as quantum entanglement. Now, the researchers say they've figured out how to turn these quantum particles' clocks forward and backward.

"In a theater, [classical physics], a movie is projected from beginning to end, regardless of what the audience wants," said Miguel Nava cues, a researcher at the Austrian Academy of Sciences' Institute of Quantum Optics and Quantum Information who worked on the research. "But at home [the quantum world], we have a remote control to manipulate the movie," he added. "We can rewind to a previous scene or skip several scenes ahead."

"We have made science fiction come true!" the researcher exclaimed. By developing a "rewind protocol," the team says they were able to revert an electron to a previous state. In experiments, they say they were able to demonstrate the use of a quantum switch to revert a photon to its original state before passing through a crystal. While it's an exciting prospect, scaling up the technique could prove extremely difficult, if not impossible.

Ref: El País; Futurism

10.Secret Corridor Discovered Inside Great Pyramid of Giza

In a recent study, cosmic rays revealed a hidden passage inside the Great Pyramid of Giza. The function of the corridor is still unknown. Scientists were able to determine its size & shape using a technique called cosmic-ray muon radiography. Of the Seven Wonders of the Ancient World, only one is left standing: the Great Pyramid, located on the Giza plateau in Egypt. Built by the pharaoh Khufu about 4,500 years ago, it was the tallest human-made building on the planet until it was eclipsed in 1889 by the Eiffel Tower. It remains an enduring testament to the ingenuity and determination of humanity. It's also an edifice shrouded in mysteries. A paper recently published in Nature Communications has lifted the veil on at least one of these mysteries. Using implacable radiation from outer space and technology first developed for use in particle accelerators, scientists collaborating with the project Scan Pyramids have discovered a new passageway inside the Great Pyramid. Researchers have been using this technique to effectively X-ray the Great Pyramid. In a recent paper, scientists found a previously unknown tunnel in the structure about 2 meters square and 9 meters long. This is not the first void found in the Great Pyramid. In 2017, some of the same researchers found an even larger void, about 30 meters long. So far, nobody knows what is in these voids. Ref: Nature Communications; Big Think

Pyramid of Giza

11. This Lens-Free Camera Is Thinner Than Human Hair

The tiny camera can switch its aperture among wide angles instantaneously. It is so thin, just a few microns thick that it could be embedded literally anywhere. For comparison, the average width of human hair is about 100 microns. The device, a square that measures just 1 by 1.2 millimeters, has the potential to switch its "aperture" among wide angle, fish eye and zoom instantaneously. And because the device is so thin, just a few microns thick, it could be embedded anywhere. (For comparison, the average width of a human hair is about 100 microns.) "The entire backside of your phone could be a camera," said Ali Haji Miri, a professor of electrical engineering and medical engineering at the California Institute of Technology (Caltech) and the principal investigator of the research paper, describing the new camera.

It could be embedded in a watch or in a pair of eyeglasses or in fabric. It could even be designed to launch into space as a small package and then unfurl into very large, thin sheets that image the universe at resolutions never before possible. "There's no fundamental limit on how much you could increase the resolution," Haji Miri said. "You could do gigapixels if you wanted." (A gigapixel image has 1 billion pixels, or 1,000 times more than an image from a 1-megapixel digital camera.) Haji Miri and his colleagues presented their innovation, called an optical phased array, at the Optical Society's (OSA) Conference on Lasers and Electro-Optics. The research was also published online in the OSA Technical Digest. The proof-of-concept device is a flat sheet with an array of 64 light receivers that can be thought of as tiny antennas tuned to receive light waves. Each receiver in the array is individually controlled by a computer program. In fractions of a second, the light receivers can be manipulated to create an image of an object on the far-right side of the view or on the far left or anywhere in between. And this can be done without pointing the device at the objects, which would be necessary with a camera. Ref: LiveScience; Caltech

Lens-Free Camera

12. First Law of Thermodynamics Has Now Been Rewritten.

The first law of thermodynamics is undergoing a huge renovation. Researchers have made a breakthrough in applying the first law to complex system. This has the potential to rewritten the way we understand complex energetic systems. Researchers at West Virginia University just released a paper detailing how the fundamental law can be applied more broadly than ever before—a finding that has the potential to rewrite the way we understand complex energetic systems.

The first law of thermodynamics is one of the bedrock laws of physics. Even if you're not gung-ho about physics research, you might have heard the simplified version: energy can neither be created nor destroyed, but it can be converted into different forms.

Suppose you heat up a balloon," said Paul Cassak, lead author on the paper, in a press release. "The first law of thermodynamics tells you how much the balloon expands and how much hotter the gas inside the balloon gets. The key is that the total amount of energy causing the balloon to expand and the gas to get hotter is the same as the amount of heat you put into the balloon." This law has been an incredibly helpful tool for physicists since its discovery in the 1850s. But there's a catch—it has historically only worked when things are in or near a state of thermodynamic equilibrium. At its core, that means the temperature of a system is consistent throughout. There aren't big hot and cold spots; it's all basically the same temperature, which means it all has pretty much the same amount of energy. Researchers have long been trying to find a way to apply the first law to systems that are not in equilibrium. The breakthrough for this team of researchers came in the form of a lot of complicated math. Basically, the energy conversion in systems that are in thermodynamic equilibrium can be described almost entirely by their density and pressure.

What the team needed was a way to quantify all of the energy conversion that wasn't described by density and pressure. And they found it. The work could have applications in fields ranging from circuitry and quantum computing to space weather. Ref: Popular Mechanics; PHYSICAL REVIEW LETTERS

13. New Anti-Dust Technology for Self-Cleaning Surfaces

Scientists have developed a new method to keep dust from sticking to surfaces. This will help make materials dust resistant, from spacecraft to solar panels to household windows with surface that can clean themselves using just gravity.

Dust is a common fact of life, and it's more than just a daily nuisance — it can get into machinery and equipment, causing loss of efficiency or breakdowns.

Researchers at The University of Texas at Austin developed

a new method to keep dust from sticking to surfaces. The result is the ability to make many types of materials dust resistant, from spacecraft to solar panels to household windows. The research is published in ACS Applied Materials & Interfaces. "What we've demonstrated here is a surface that can clean itself," said Chih-Hao Chang, an associate professor in the Cockrell School of Engineering's Walker Department of Mechanical Engineering and a lead author of the study. "Particulates aren't able to stick to the surface, so they come off using just the force of gravity."

In tests, the researchers piled lunar dust on top of their engineered surfaces and then turned each surface on its side. The result: Only about 2% of the surface remained dusty, compared with more than 35% of a similarly smooth surface. The researchers said the discovery boils down to things the human eye can't detect. In the experiments, the team altered the geometry of flat surfaces to create a tightly packed nanoscale network of pyramid-shaped structures. These sharp, angular structures make it difficult for the dust particles to stick to the material, instead sticking to one another and rolling off the material via gravity. Ref: phys.org; ACS

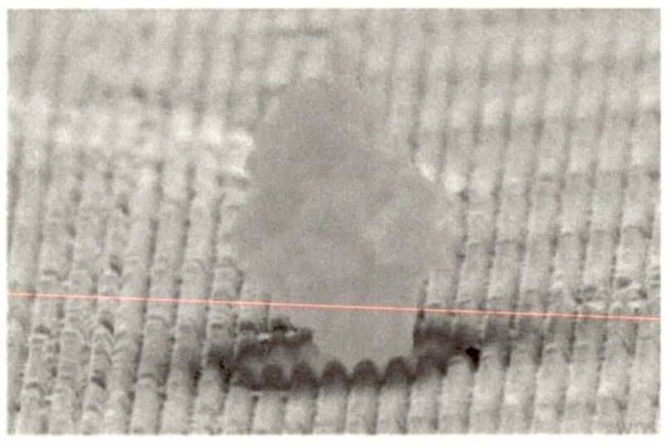

Anti-Dust Technology

14.Cancer-Fighting Army

Magnetically controlled swarms of microscopic robots will soon help fight cancer inside the body. Scientists have developed a way to magnetic robots embedded within injectable microscopic pills to perform specific and unique tasks. Over the past decade, scientists have shown they can manipulate magnetic forces to guide medical devices within the human body, as these fields can apply forces to remotely control objects. For instance, prior work used magnetic fields to maneuver a catheter inside the heart and steer video capsules in the gut.

Previous research also used magnetic fields to simultaneously control swarms of tiny magnets. In principle, these objects could work together on large problems such as fighting cancers. However, individually guiding members of a team of microscopic devices so that each move in its own direction and at its own speed remains a challenge. This is because identical magnetic items under the control of the same magnetic field usually behave identically to each other.

Recently, scientists developed a way to magnetically control each member of a swarm of magnetic devices to perform specific, unique tasks. "Our method may enable complex manipulations inside the human body," said study lead author Jürgen Rahmer, a physicist at Philips Innovative Technologies in Hamburg, Germany. First, the scientists created a number of tiny identical magnetic screws. The researchers next used a strong, uniform magnetic field to freeze groups of these magnetic screws in place. In small, weak spots within this powerful magnetic field, the microscopic screws are free to move. Superimposing a relatively weak rotating magnetic field could make these free screws spin.

In experiments, the researchers could make several magnetic screws whirl in different directions at the same time with pinpoint accuracy. In principle, the scientists noted, they could manipulate hundreds of microscopic robots at once.

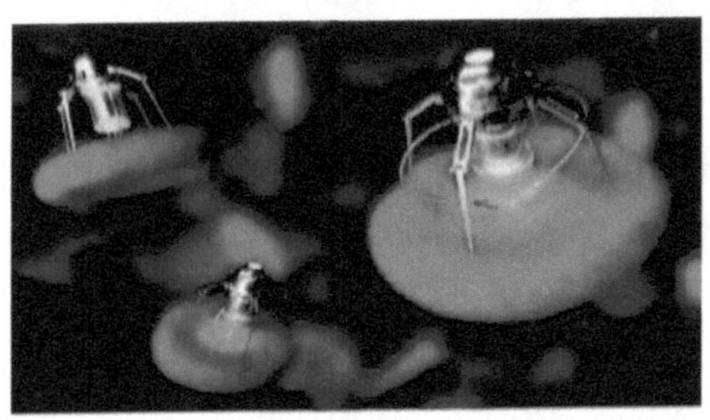

Microscopic Robots

15. What is Mission Chandrayaan-4

The mission will be launched in two phases onboard two LVM3 rockets. The spacecraft will have five modules packed into two composites which are launched separately. The lander module with the ascender module attached on its top and supported by a propulsion module beneath it will be a single composite, while the transfer module along with the re-entry module will be another composite. The spacecraft will get assembled into an integrated module by docking in Earth orbit before proceeding to the Moon

Propulsion Module is similar to the propulsion module on Chandrayaan-3. It will ferry the combined modular spacecraft to the moon Lander Module will land on the

Moon with instrumentation. It supports the ascend stage along with the soil sampling instrumentation. It is designed to last 1 lunar day or 14 earth days on the moon. Ascender Module will eject from the lander and would launch from the Moon using the lander as a launch pad after the samples from the Moon are collected and stored. It will then enter low-lunar orbit Transfer Module will collect the samples from the ascend stage, transfer them to the re-entry module, fire its engine to set both itself and the re-entry module towards Earth, release the payload and loop back around the Earth. Re-entry Module will hold the sample from lunar orbit. It is designed to survive atmospheric re-entry and land with the lunar regoliths. Apart from the propulsion module, the transfer module is also equipped with an onboard Liquid Apogee Motor (LAM) for return operation manoeuvres including the trans-Earth injection. As per earlier reports, the lander module will have six throttleable landing thrusters capable of producing 800 newtons of thrust each, while the ascender module will have two lift off thrusters capable of producing 800 newtons of fixed thrust each. The integrated assembly of all modules after docking in Earth orbit is expected to weigh at least 6,727 kg (14,830 lb)

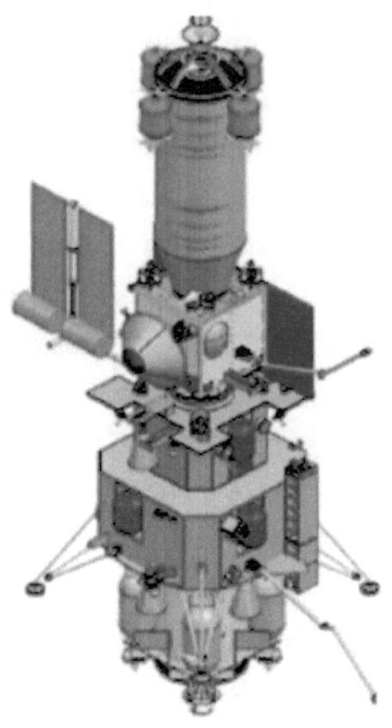

Chandrayaan-4

16. "MOLECULE" Of Light

Ever thought of light as a molecule? The first molecule made from two photons was created in 2013. In 2018, scientists also created a "photon triplet" by firing pair of photons through an ultracold atomic gas, where an attractive interaction causes the photons to stick and becomes quantum-mechanically entangled. Getting photons to stick together is not easy because they normally pass through each other without interacting. However, a photon has an associated electromagnetic field that can modify its surrounding medium.

These changes can affect nearby photons and create an effective interaction between them. Although this effect is usually tiny, the interactions can be significant if the medium is chosen carefully. A team at Harvard University and the Massachusetts Institute of Technology had created strong interactions between photons by sending them through a gas of rubidium atoms chilled to a temperature of just a few degrees above absolute zero. The experiment involved using blue laser light with a carefully chosen wavelength of 479nm, which modifies the rubidium atoms so that a photon can share some of its energy with several atoms and create a collective "Rydberg state".

This state is like a Rydberg atom – in which an electron is promoted to a very high-energy state but instead, the electron is shared among several atoms.

This Rydberg state propagates through the gas like a sluggish photon with a non-zero mass and when the collective state reaches the opposite edge of the gas cloud, the photon re-emerges at its original energy.

When a Rydberg state forms, however, it becomes impossible for more Rydberg states to be created nearby, thanks to a process called the Rydberg blockade. So, when two photons are fired into the gas in quick succession, the first forms a Rydberg state but the second does not. As far as the second photon is concerned, the region of the Rydberg state has a different index of refraction than the rest of the gas, which causes the second photon to stay close to the first as they travel together through the gas. The result is a bound state of two photons – or a molecule – traveling through the atomic gas. Ref: Physics World;

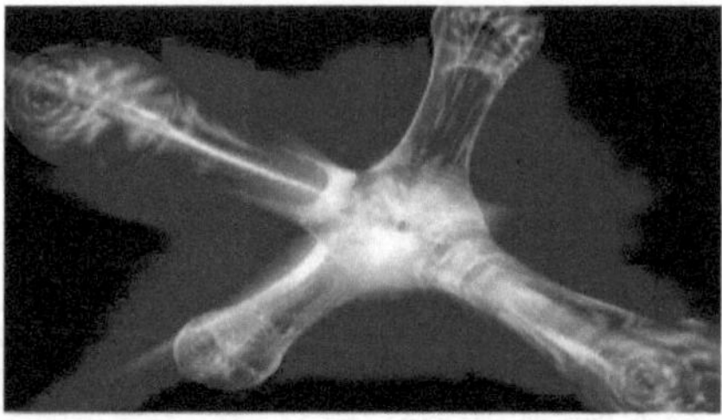

17.Dragonfly On Titan

Saturn's moon Titan has long intrigued astronomers with its thick atmosphere and lakes of methane. It's the only moon in our Solar system that has a dense atmosphere. A rover- size drone called Dragonfly is expected to launch for this moon in 2027 to study possibility of any life there.

"It's the first drone lander and it can fly over 100 miles through Titan's thick atmosphere," said former NASA Administrator Jim Bridenstine in a statement. "Titan is most comparable to early Earth. Dragonfly's instruments will help evaluate organic chemistry and the chemical signatures of past or present life. We will launch Dragonfly to explore the frontiers of human knowledge for the benefit of all humanity."

The ultimate goal is for Dragonfly to visit an impact crater, where they believe that important ingredients for life mixed together when something hit Titan in the past, possibly tens of thousands of years ago. It's a Mars rover-sized drone, reaching about ten feet long.

Titan is similar chemically to Earth before life evolved, the agency said. They want to explore sand dunes on Titan to determine if they're made of the same complex organic material discovered in the atmosphere.

"Titan has the key ingredients for life," said Lori Glaze, director of NASA's Planetary Science Division. "It has complex organic molecules and the energy required for life. We will have the opportunity to observe processes similar to what happened on early Earth when life formed and potentially conditions that could harbor life today. We can look for biosignatures."

Once Dragonfly lands, it will spend two and a half years flying around Titan. It only has propellers, with skids to land, but no wheels to allow it to roam over the surface.

Dragonfly

18. This Device Can Produce Light Using Just Seawater

A company named E-Dina has developed a lantern that can produce light using only seawater. This little device "water Light" can take half a liter of salt water and produce 45 days of light. It has a lifetime of around 5600 hours.

It may be difficult to believe, but a shocking number of people in the world do not have access to electricity. There are around 770 million people in the world with no electricity in 2023, mostly living in the global south. That's just under 10% of all people on Earth. One innovation that could help provide power to those currently without it is courtesy of a Colombian company named E-Dina, which has developed a lantern that can produce light using only seawater.

Named Water Light, the smart little device can take half a liter of salt water and produce an impressive 45 days of light. The energy comes from an electrochemical reaction between the salt water and a magnesium electrode inside the Water Light, generating an electric current.

As well as being built entirely from recycled materials, the lanterns can also provide energy to charge small electronic devices. It has an impressive lifetime, too, lasting for 5,600 hours, which is longer than incandescent or halogen lightbulbs. For those who don't live near the sea, a Water Light can even produce energy from urine. Ref: Grunge; IEA; E-Dina

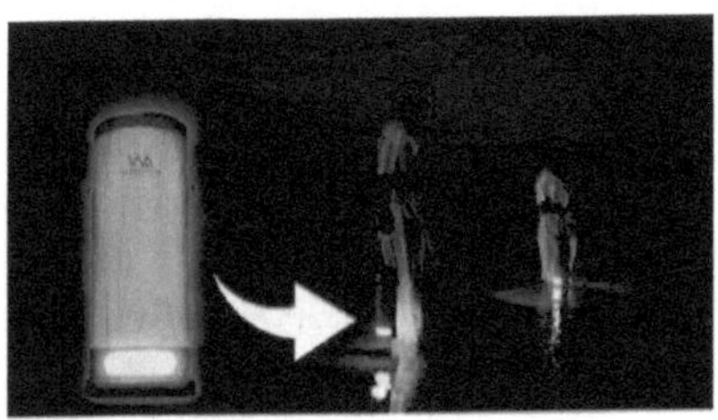

19.The Dark Photons

Observations suggest that the intergalactic gas in our universe is a little hotter than it should be. Recently, astrophysicists have used computer an exotic form of dark matter known as "dark photon" could be heating the cosmos.

The universe is slightly hotter than it should be. 'Dark photons' could be to blame. These strange particles would be the carriers of a new, fifth force of nature that normal matter does not experience, but occasionally these dark photons can flip their identities to become regular photons, providing a source of heat. We could find such dark photons by observing the intergalactic gas using what's known as the Lyman-alpha Forest. When we observe light from a distant, bright object, like a quasar (glowing objects powered by black holes at the centers of distant galaxies), there is a series of gaps in an otherwise smooth spectrum of light from that faraway object. Here's why: that light has to filter through billions of light-years of gas to reach us. Occasionally that light will pass through a relatively dense clump of neutral hydrogen — a type of hydrogen that consists of one proton and one neutron, and which permeates gas clouds throughout the universe. Most of that light will pass through unaffected, but a very specific wavelength of light will get absorbed. This wavelength corresponds to the energy difference needed to bump an electron from its first to its second energy level inside the hydrogen atoms.

This is a very hypothetical form of dark matter, the mysterious, invisible substance that accounts for roughly 80% of all the mass in the universe, yet doesn't seem to interact with light. Since astronomers do not currently understand the identity of dark matter, the field is wide open with possibilities as to what it could be. In this model, instead of the dark matter being made of invisible particles (like a phantom version of electrons, for example), it would instead be made of a new kind of force carrier — that is, a type of particle that mediates interactions between other particles.

Source Ref: LiveScience

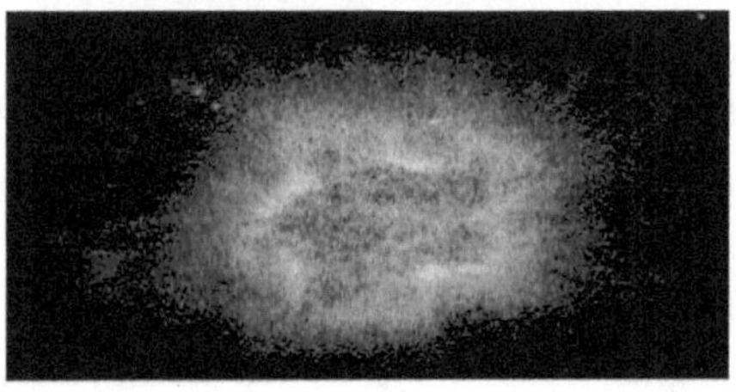

Dark Photons

20. The Antimatter Trap

To study antimatter, you need to prevent it from annihilating with the matter. Charged anti-particles like positrons can be held in penning traps that are comparable to tiny accelerators in which particles spiral around as the magnetic and electric fields keep them from colliding with the walls of the trap. Scientists have created ways to store antimatter and prevent it from annihilating with matter. But Penning traps won't work on neutral particles such as antihydrogen. Because they have no charge, these particles cannot be confined by electric fields.

Instead, they are held in Joffe traps, which work by creating a region of space where the magnetic field gets larger in all directions. The particle gets stuck in the area with the weakest magnetic field, much like a marble rolling around the bottom of a bowl.

We have explained the discovery, production, storage, and the entire physics of Antimatter in a detailed video. Please

check it out. Link is in our bio!
Ref Source: CERN

Antimatter Trap

21. 6th State of Matters

A fermionic condensate (or Fermi–Dirac condensate) is a superfluid phase formed by fermionic particles at low temperatures. It is closely related to the Bose–Einstein condensate, a superfluid phase formed by bosonic atoms under similar conditions. The earliest recognized fermionic condensate described the state of electrons in a superconductor; the physics of other examples including recent work with fermionic atoms is analogous. The first atomic fermionic condensate was created by a team led by Deborah S. Jin using potassium-40 atoms at the University of Colorado Boulder in 2003 It is far more difficult to produce a fermionic superfluid than a bosonic one, because the Pauli exclusion principle prohibits fermions from occupying the same quantum state. However, there is a well-known mechanism by which a superfluid may be formed from fermions: That mechanism is the BCS transition, discovered in 1957 by J. Bardeen, L.N. Cooper, and R. Schrieffer for describing superconductivity. These authors showed that, below a certain temperature, electrons (which are fermions) can pair up to form bound pairs now known as Cooper pairs. As long as collisions with the ionic lattice of the solid do not supply enough energy to break the Cooper pairs, the electron fluid will be able to flow without dissipation. As a result, it becomes a superfluid, and the material through which it flows a superconductor.

The BCS theory was phenomenally successful in describing superconductors. Soon after the publication of the BCS paper, several theorists proposed that a similar phenomenon could occur in fluids made up of fermions other than electrons, such as helium-3 atoms. These speculations were confirmed in 1971, when experiments performed by D.D. Osheroff showed that helium-3 becomes a superfluid below 0.0025 K. It was soon verified that the superfluidity of helium-3 arises from a BCS-like mechanism

Beyond solid, liquid, and gas: the 7 states of matter

Most of us, on Earth, have a familiarity with three phases of matter: solids, liquids and gases. But at higher temperatures, the atoms making up matter ionize, creating a plasma, and at really high temperatures, individual protons and neutrons break down into a quark-gluon plasma.

Meanwhile, at very low temperatures, the different types of particles form either Bose-Einstein or Fermionic condensates. All told, there are 7 known states of matter, not merely three.

How many states of matter are there? When you were young, you probably learned about the three that are most common to our experience: solid, liquid, and gas. All of these occur with regularity here on Earth's surface: rocks and ices are solids, water and many oils are liquids, while the atmosphere that we breathe is a gas. However, these three common states of matter are all based on neutral atoms; restrictions that the Universe is not bound by.If you bombard any atom with enough energy, you'll kick the electrons off of it, creating an ionized plasma: the fourth state of matter. Turn up the energy high enough, and even protons and neutrons will disintegrate, forming a quark-gluon plasma: arguably the fifth state of matter. But there are two additional states of matter that not only can exist, but do: Bose-Einstein Condensates and Fermionic Condensates, the sixth and seventh states of matter. At present, they're only achievable under extreme laboratory conditions, but they might play an important role in the Universe itself. Here's why.

Here on Earth, everything is made up of atoms. Some atoms bind together to form molecules; other atoms exist as standalone entities. Regardless of the number of atoms in any particular chemical compound — water, oxygen, methane, helium, etc. — the combination of temperature and pressure conditions determines whether it's a solid, liquid, or gas.Water, most famously, freezes at low temperatures and modest pressures, becomes liquid at either higher pressures and/or higher temperatures, and becomes a gas at still higher temperatures or very low pressures. There's a critical temperature, however, above about 374 °C (705 °F), at which this distinction breaks down. At low pressures, you still get a gas; at higher pressures, you get a supercritical fluid with properties of both gas and liquid. Go to higher temperatures still, and you'll begin ionizing your molecules, creating a plasma: that fourth state of matter.

8th State Of Matters

Hexatic State: -

Definition: The hexatic state is an intermediate phase between the solid and isotropic liquid phases in two-dimensional systems of particles.

Characteristics: In this state, particles exhibit short-range positional order like a liquid but maintain long-range orientational order similar to a solid.

Discovery: This state was theorized and later observed in systems such as thin films and colloidal suspensions

9th State of Matters

Quark-Gluon Plasma

Definition: Quark-Gluon Plasma (QGP) is a state of matter in which quarks and gluons, which are normally confined within protons and neutrons, are free to move independently.

Conditions: This state occurs at extremely high temperatures and energy densities, such as those found in the early universe just microseconds after the Big Bang.

Discovery: QGP has been created and studied in particle accelerators like the Large Hadron Collider (LHC) and the Relativistic Heavy Ion Collider (RHIC).

Characteristics

High Energy: QGP exists at temperatures exceeding trillions of degrees Celsius, far hotter than the core of the sun.

Strong Interaction: It provides insights into the strong force, one of the four fundamental forces of nature, which binds quarks together within protons and neutrons.This state of matter is crucial for understanding the fundamental properties of the universe and the behaviour of matter under extreme conditions

10th State of Matters

The tenth state of matter is known as Rydberg Matter.

Definition: Rydberg matter is a phase of matter formed by Rydberg atoms, which are atoms with one or more electrons in highly excited states.

Formation: It occurs when these excited atoms cluster together, creating a unique state with properties distinct from other known states of matter.

Characteristics: Rydberg matter exhibits long-range interactions and can form at relatively low temperatures.This state of matter is fascinating because it provides insights into the behavior of atoms in highly excited states and their interactions.

11th State of Matters

The eleventh state of matter is known as Photonic Matter.

Photonic Matter

Definition: Photonic matter is a state where photons, which are typically massless particles of light, interact with each other in such a way that they behave as if they have mass.

Formation: This state is achieved under specific conditions where photons are made to interact strongly with each other, often using a medium like a cold atomic gas.

Characteristics: In this state, photons can form bound states, creating structures similar to molecules.This state of matter is fascinating because it challenges our traditional understanding of light and matter, opening up new possibilities in quantum computing and other advanced technologies.

22. The Big Rip Theory

*The **Big Rip Theory** proposes that the expansion of our Universe will continue to acceleration, eventually leading to **complete destruction** of all structures, including galaxies, stars, planets, and even atoms. This could happen in the next **22 billion years.***

his theory is based on the idea that the expansion of the universe is driven by a mysterious force called dark energy, which is thought to make up about 68% of the universe's total energy density. According to the Big Rip theory, as the expansion of the universe continues to accelerate, the gravitational pull between celestial bodies will weaken. This will cause galaxies, stars, and planets to fly apart, and eventually, the expansion will become so fast that it will overcome the forces that hold atoms and molecules together, causing them to disintegrate

The Big Rip theory predicts that this process will happen in a finite amount of time, known as the "time to the rip", which is estimated to be around 22 billion years.

The Big Rip theory is one of several proposed explanations for the ultimate fate of the universe, and it is still under debate among scientists.

There is evidence that dark energy is accelerating the expansion of the universe, but the exact nature of dark energy is not well understood, and it is still uncertain whether its density will continue to increase or remain constant. It's also important to note that the Big Rip theory is based on certain assumptions and it is not the only explanation for the ultimate fate of the universe. Other theories such as the Big Crunch or the Big Freeze also propose different outcomes for the fate of the universe.

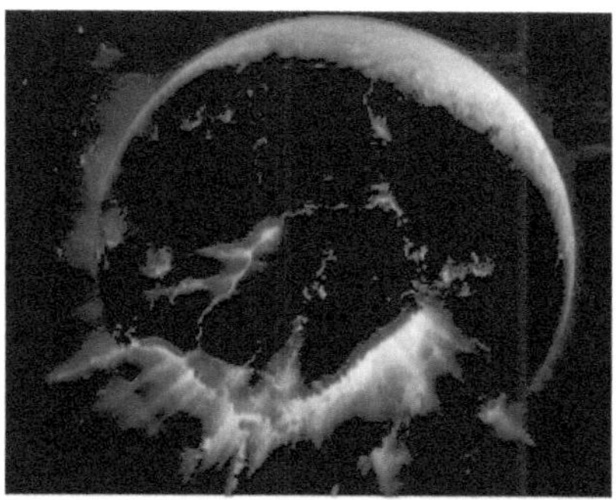

23. Scientists Turned an Entire Room into Wireless Charger

*In 2017, researchers at **The Walt Disney Company** supersized the wireless technology by building a **wireless charging room** that can boost batteries of 10 objects simultaneously. The researchers said they ware **inspired by inventor Nikola Tesla.***

Scientists at a branch of The Walt Disney Company called Disney Research converted an entire room into a wireless charger that can boost the batteries of 10 objects at one time. The researchers said they were inspired by inventor Nikola Tesla, who created the first system to wirelessly transmit electricity — the Tesla coil. Tesla believed there could be a global network of wireless electricity that would use an electromagnetic wave that reverberated between the ionosphere (a layer of the Earth's atmosphere filled with ions and free electrons) and the ground, study co-author Alanson Sample, an associate lab director and principal research scientist at Disney Research, explained in a video. While Tesla's vision didn't come to fruition, Sample and his colleagues were inspired to investigate how wireless charging could be set up in large spaces. "What we really want is a three-dimensional charging experience, where you walk into your living room or office and your cellphone is charged simply by walking in," Sample said in the video. "We have a metalized room, and we're going to use standing electromagnetic waves that reverberate all around this room, providing wireless power to any devices inside." Known as quasistatic cavity resonance (QSCR), the wireless charging technology uses electromagnetic fields generated by electrical currents. Disney Research's room is outfitted with aluminum-paneled walls and a centrally located copper pole that houses 15 capacitors (which store electrical energy, as batteries do).

As the capacitors generate electrical currents, they travel through the ceiling, walls, and floor, and then back through the pole. These electrical currents create the electromagnetic fields that circulate around the pole and wirelessly charge devices in the room.

Source: journal PLOS ONE

Wireless Charger

24. Plant Spark with Electricity During Thunderstorm's.

*During electricity storms, plants sometimes react to the electrical fields caused by the storms by discharging **tiny sparks of electricity**. These sparks can create a faint blue haze known as a **corona**. Weirdly, this discharge may **affect air quality**.*

Scientists have long been aware that plants and trees can emit small, visible electric discharges from the tips of their leaves when the plants are trapped beneath the electrical fields generated by thunderstorms high overhead. These discharges, known as coronas, are sometimes visible as faint, blue sparks that glow around charged objects. Weirdly, these discharges may affect air quality. In a 2022 study published in the Journal of Geophysical Research: Atmospheres, researchers found that coronas produced high levels of highly reactive chemicals called radicals. Radicals lack electrons and can steal them from nearby atoms, thus altering the chemical compounds around them. This may remove some harmful compounds from the air, but may also create new air pollutants as well, the researchers reported. The two radicals given off by the plant coronas are hydroxyl (OH) and hydroperoxyl (HO2), both of which are negatively charged and are known to oxidize, or steal electrons from, a number of different chemical compounds, thereby transforming them into other molecules. The researchers were particularly interested in the concentrations of hydroxyl radicals because they have a greater impact on air quality. Source: Journal of Geophysical Research: Atmospheres

Electric plant

25. This Airplane Wing Can Change Its Shape Mid-Air

__NASA with MIT__ built and tested a radically new kind of airplane wings, assembled from hundreds of tiny identical pieces. These wings can __change their shape mid-air__ to control the plane in unfavorable wind conditions and provide better efficiency.

The Mission Adaptive Digital Composite Aerostructure Technologies, or MADCAT, at NASA's Ames Research Center in California's Silicon Valley, uses carbon fiber composites — a strong and light material made of carbon atoms to design and test efficient, ultra-light wings that can adapt on the fly.

Advanced carbon fiber composite materials are used to create "blocks," modular units that can be arranged in repeating lattice-based patterns. It includes the same crisscrossing patterns you might see in a garden fence or even a cherry pie. This variation in patterns creates a structure that can precisely flex and adapt. Computers integrated into the wing use algorithms to help it morph and twist into the most efficient shape mid-flight. Source: nasaames

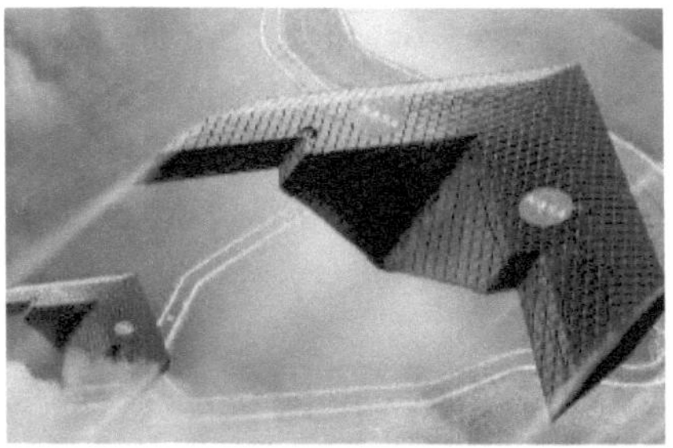

Airplane Wing

26. The Ghost Particle

*Neutrinos are the **most abundant particles** that have mass in the universe. Every time any atomic nuclei come together or break apart, they produce neutrinos. Once produced, these ghostly particles almost **never interact with other matter**. Tens of trillions of neutrinos from the sun stream through your body every second, but you can't feel them.*

Every time atomic nuclei come together (like in the sun) or break apart (like in a nuclear reactor), they produce neutrinos. Even a banana emits neutrinos; they come from the natural radioactivity of the potassium in the fruit.

Once produced, these ghostly particles almost never interact with other matter. Tens of trillions of neutrinos from the sun stream through your body every second, but you can't feel them. Theorists predicted the neutrino's existence in 1930, but it took experimenters 26 years to discover the particle. Today, scientists are trying to determine the neutrino's mass, how it interacts with matter, and whether the neutrino is its own antiparticle (a particle with the same mass but opposite electric or magnetic properties) or not. Some scientists think neutrinos might be why all antimatter (the antiparticles of all matter) disappeared after the Big Bang, leaving us in a universe made of matter. Info Source: Fermi National Accelerator Laboratory, DOE

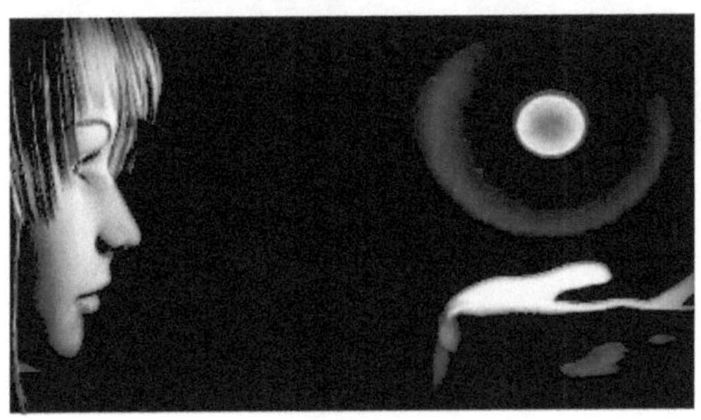

Ghost Particle

27.The Higgs Boson

*The **Higgs boson** is the fundamental force-carrying particle of the Higgs fields. Which is responsible for grating other particles their mass. The Higgs boson has a mass of **125 billion electron volts,** meaning it is 130 times more massive than a proton. The Higgs Boson is the only elementary particle **with no spin.***

The Higgs boson is the fundamental particle associated with the Higgs field, a field that gives mass to other fundamental particles such as electrons and quarks.
A particle's mass determines how much it resists changing its speed or position when it encounters a force. Not all fundamental particles have mass. The photon, which is the particle of light and carries the electromagnetic force, has

no mass at all. The Higgs boson was proposed in 1964 by Peter Higgs, François Englert, and four other theorists to explain why certain particles have mass. Scientists confirmed its existence in 2012 through the ATLAS and CMS experiments at the Large Hadron Collider (LHC) at CERN in Switzerland. This discovery led to the 2013 Nobel Prize in Physics being awarded to Higgs and Englert. Scientists are now studying the characteristic properties of the Higgs boson to determine if it precisely matches the predictions of the Standard Model of particle physics. If the Higgs boson deviates from the model, it may provide clues to new particles that only interact with other Standard Model particles through the Higgs boson and thereby lead to new scientific discoveries. Source: CERN; DOE

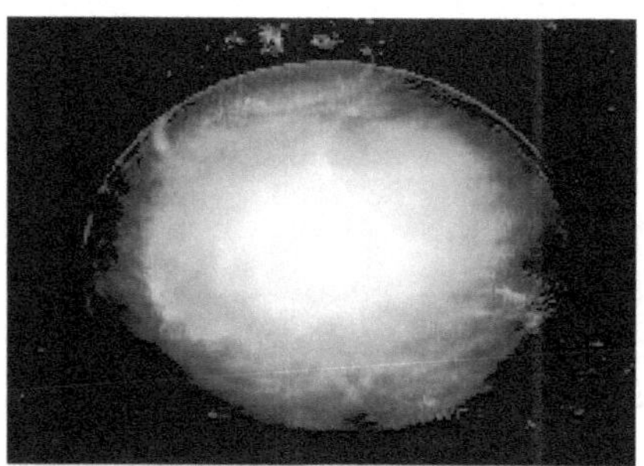

Higgs Boson

28. Bird That Has Dinosaur-Like Head, Discovered in China

Scientists have unearthed the fossil of a bizarre creature in China dating back to 120 million years that has the head of a dinosaur and the body of a bird, further complicating the debate

whether birds are the descendants of dinosaurs.

A bizarre creature that lived in China around 120 million years ago had a dinosaur's head and a bird's body; a study published in Nature Ecology & Evolution revealed. Researchers at the Chinese Academy of Sciences (CAS) studied the recently discovered complete fossil of the creature named Cratonavis zhui. They found that the chicken-sized hybrid had long shoulder blades and claws, but its large skull was shaped in an almost identical way to that of T-Rex and other meat-eating theropods. The researchers studied the fossil by using high-resolution computed tomography, or CT scans. This enabled them to digitally manipulate the specimen's bones and reconstruct the original shape of the skull, and even deduce some of its dinosaur-related functions. According to the study, the team also analyzed Cratonavis' shoulder blade and metatarsal, a long bone in the foot that connects the ankle to the toes, in order to understand more about its birdlike body. They confirmed that the creature's skull is morphologically nearly identical to those of dinosaurs, rather than those of standard birds.

Standard Birds

29. Plastic-like material that conducts like metal.

Scientists have discovered a way to create a material that can be made like Plastic, but conducts electricity more like a metal. It can be painted, sprayed or even molded into any shape. This goes against all

A plastic material that has metallic properties and remains stable even when heated, chilled, left in the air or exposed to acid has been revealed, with researchers saying it could prove valuable in wearable electronics. What's more, the material can be made into any shape, the researchers say. "It's a dark black powder. However, when we put it on a surface as a film, or press it like Play-Doh, it becomes iridescent and shiny," said Dr John Anderson, senior author of the research from the University of Chicago. "From what we can tell, it's stable up to [about] 250 degrees Celsius," he added, noting the material has a conductivity similar to graphite.

Electrical conductivity occurs in materials in which electrons can flow freely. But it has traditionally been thought that a key feature of solid conductive materials is an ordered structure. However, the new substance, a metallopolymer formed of chains of molecules made of Sulphur, carbon and hydrogen that carry nickel at regular intervals, has been shown to be highly conductive, despite being amorphous. The team say there isn't a solid theory to explain the material's properties. But writing in the journal Nature, the researchers say they think chains of polymer form disordered stacks. One way of thinking about this is to imagine a messy pile of playing cards. The stacks pack together in a disordered fashion, creating a material that is amorphous but still allows electrons to flow both horizontally and vertically.

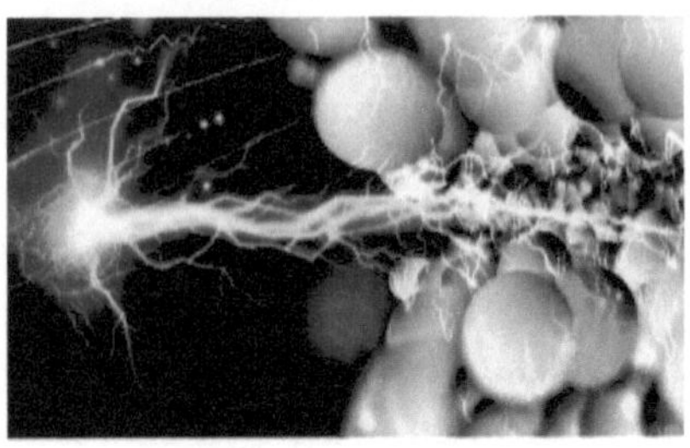

Plastic Like Material

30. 'Lunar-Brick' Made of Moondust & Salt Water

*Scientists have created **3D-printed bricks** using lunar regolith (dust and loose rocks from the lunar surface) that may be used to construct future lunar bases. The researchers found that these bricks could **withstand 250 million times the Earth's atmospheric pressure.***

NASA aims to establish a permanent presence on the moon with its Artemis program and its asked scientists to devise clever new methods for building lunar bases capable of withstanding the harsh conditions of our nearest cosmic neighbor. Now, thanks to experiments run by scientists at the University of Central Florida (UCF), future lunar astronauts could use bricks made of lunar regolith and saltwater to build their homes. Ranajay Ghosh, associate professor of UCF's Department of Mechanical and Aerospace Engineering, and a team discovered that 3D-printed bricks made using lunar regolith — dust and loose rocks from the lunar surface — are capable of withstanding the extreme conditions of the moon.

The researchers created the bricks using a combination of 3D printing and binder jet technology (BJT) an additive manufacturing method in which a liquid binding agent is deposited on a bed of powder particles. "BJT is uniquely suitable for ceramic-like materials that are difficult to melt with a laser," Ghosh explained. "Therefore, it has great potential for regolith-based extraterrestrial manufacturing in a sustainable way to produce parts, components, and construction structures." In their BJT experiment, the researchers used saltwater as the binding agent, and the powder was a substitute for lunar regolith. These bricks could withstand pressures of up to 250 million times the Earth's atmosphere. Last year, a University of Manchester scientist proposed using human blood and urine as a binding agent for future housing on Mars. They stated this would significantly reduce the cost and increase the speed of construction for future off-world colonies and that astronauts, though the health implications still need to be investigated.

'Lunar-Brick'

31. Scientists Found Mysterious Diamond from Outer Space

*Researchers think that a dwarf planet and a **sizable asteroid** collided approximately 4.5 billion years ago, resulting in the formation of the diamond. The unusual hexagonal structure the diamond could make it harder than **most diamonds on Earth.***

Researchers from Australia and the United Kingdom have revealed in a recent study that a strange diamond from an ancient dwarf planet found its way to Earth's surface.

The revelation started to unfold when geologist Andy Tomkins, a professor at Monash University in Australia, was out in the field categorizing meteorites. He came across a strange "bended" kind of diamond in a space rock in Northwest Africa, said study coauthor Alan Salek, a doctoral student, and researcher at RMIT University in Australia. After more investigation, it was discovered that the meteorite included lonsdaleite, a rare hexagonal stone. According to research, Lonsdaleite is thought to have been produced "from a supercritical fluid at a high temperature and moderate pressure,".

In an article published by RMIT University, one of the research partners, Tomkins was quoted as saying, "Later, lonsdaleite was partially replaced by a diamond as the environment cooled and the pressure decreased,".

Researchers believe that the dwarf planet and a sizable asteroid collided approximately 4.5 billion years ago, resulting in the formation of the diamond.

The unusual hexagonal structure of the diamond could make it harder than most diamonds originating from Earth. It has been discovered that lonsdaleite may be tougher than typical diamonds, which have a cubic structure. According to academics, its peculiar creation may have significant technological applications.

Although it is normal to conceive of diamonds as having formed under the extreme pressures present deep inside the Earth, some of the strongest jewels have also been discovered in meteorites, and they are fundamentally distinct from their terrestrial counterparts.

hexagonal structure diamond

32. Scientists Have Created a Material That Can "Think"

*Scientists have created the first example of an **engineering material** that can simultaneously sense, think and act without requiring additional circuits to process such signals, similar to the **brain's role in the human body**.*

Someone taps your shoulder. The organized touch receptors in your skin send a message to your brain, which processes the information and directs you to look left, in the direction of the tap. Now, Penn State and U.S. Air Force researchers have harnessed this processing of mechanical information and integrated it into engineered materials that "think".

The work hinges on a novel, reconfigurable alternative to integrated circuits. Integrated circuits are typically composed of multiple electronic components housed on a single semiconductor material, usually silicon, and they run all types of modern electronics, including phones, cars and robots. Integrated circuits are scientists' realization of information processing similar to the brain's role in the human body. Integrated circuits are the core constituent needed for scalable computing of signals and information but have never before been realized by scientists in any composition other than silicon semiconductors. This discovery revealed the opportunity for nearly any material around us to act like its own integrated circuit: being able to "think" about what's happening around it. The soft polymer material acts like a brain that can receive digital strings of information that are then processed, resulting in new sequences of digital information that can control reactions.

"Thinking " Material

33. World's Strongest Magnetic Field Generated in China

Chinese scientists have set a world record for the strongest steady magnetic field ever generated on Earth. The hybrid magnet produced a field of 45.22 Tesla, which is more than a million times stronger than Earth's magnetic field

The magnetic field facility is not much bigger than a coin, with a diameter of 33mm. But the Chinese Academy of Sciences' High Magnetic Field Laboratory says it can create a stable magnetic field as strong as 45.22 tesla – or over a million times stronger than that of the Earth. The original world record was created by the National High Magnetic Field Laboratory in the United States in 1999. Its hybrid magnet generated 450,000 gauss [45 tesla] and it has held the record for 23 years. Generating such a powerful magnetic field is challenging, partly because it requires a huge amount of energy, and the force is strong enough to lift an aircraft carrier.

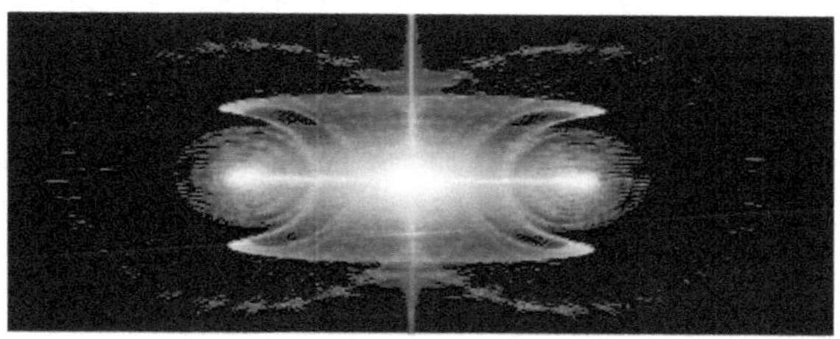

High Magnetic Field

34. This New Robot Can Travel to Black Holes!

*Researcher developed a new robot that could help us **travel around black**. The robot recreates the same **environment found around black holes**. It does so by moving in a curved space, and thus defying the laws of physics.*

When humans, animals, and machines move throughout the world, they always push against something, such as the ground, air, or water. Until recently, physicists thought this to be a constant, following the law of conservation momentum.

However, scientists from the Georgia Institute of Technology (Georgia Tech) have now proven the opposite – when bodies exist in curved spaces, it turns out that they can in fact move without pushing against something.

In the paper, a team of scientists created a robot confined to a spherical surface with unprecedented levels of isolation from its environment, so that these curvature-induced effects would predominate. "We let our shape-changing object move on the simplest curved space, a sphere, to systematically study the motion in curved space," said lead researcher. "We learned that the predicted effect, which was so counter-intuitive it was dismissed by some physicists, indeed occurred: as the robot changed its shape, it inched forward around the sphere in a way that could not be attributed to environmental interactions." Although the effects are small, as robotics becomes increasingly precise, understanding this curvature-induced effect may be of practical importance, just as the slight frequency shift induced by gravity became crucial to allow GPS systems to accurately convey their positions to orbital satellites. Ultimately, the principles of how a space's curvature can be harnessed for locomotion may allow spacecraft to navigate the highly curved space around a black hole.

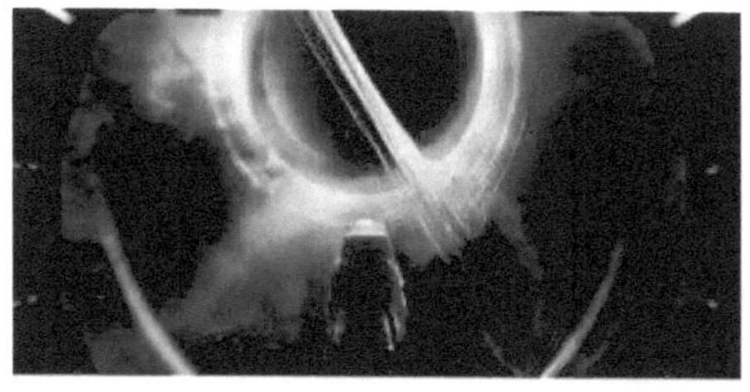

New Robot

Scientific Discovery

1.Scientists Discovered New Layer Inside Earth's Core.

Geography textbooks will have to be rewritten as scientists have confirmed that the earth is made up of five, not four, layers. They have discovered about – the innermost inner core. We've all seen the cross-sectional diagrams of the Earth which show its four layers: the crust, the mantle, the outer core, and the inner core. It seems these diagrams are incomplete. Seismologists at Australian National University (ANU) used data from about 200 earthquakes of magnitude 6 or higher to dive deep into Earth's innards and rewrite what we thought we knew.

Measuring the different speeds at which the waves travelled through the planet, the scientists were able to map out the Earth's inner structure and found that there is an additional distinct layer deep within.

This solid "metallic ball" sits within the inner core and is known as the "innermost inner core."

As the innermost inner core likely contains information from millions, even billions, of years ago, the discovery may help us understand how our planet formed.

"The existence of an internal metallic ball within the inner core, the innermost inner core, was hypothesized about 20 years ago," says ANU's Dr. Thanh-Son Pham. "We now provide another line of evidence to prove the hypothesis."

Ref source: Cosmos magazine; AN

2.Scientists Discovered The Darkest Planet

TrES-2b called "the planet of eternal night" bounces back less than 1% of the light it receives from its star. In facts the planet reflects less light than charcoal or black acrylic paint, which absorbs nearly all light. The air of this planet is as hot as lava. It's a mystery as to what's causing it to be so dark.

TrES-2b is lurking around the yellow sun-like star GSC 03549-02811 some 750 light-years away in the direction of the constellation Draco.

TrES-2b apparently lacks reflective clouds, super-heated as its atmosphere is to more than 980 degrees Celsius by a star just 5 million kilometers away from it. It's so hot that it emits a faint red glow, much like a burning ember or the coils on an electric stove. The researchers propose that light-absorbing chemicals such as vaporized sodium and potassium or gaseous titanium oxide in the planet's atmosphere could help explain why it is so dark. Still, none of these can fully explain why the world is as stealthily cloaked as it is.

3.Something Very Strange Is Happening on Saturn

NASA has confirmed that a new "spoke season" is kicking off at Saturn. These are the times of the Saturnian Year when mysterious radial smudge marks appear across the planet's rings. What exactly causes these spokes is unknown.

The Hubble Space Telescope has confirmed that a new "spoke season" is kicking off at Saturn. These are the times of the Saturnian year, centered around the equinoxes, when mysterious radial smudge marks, like the spokes of a wheel, appear across the planet's rings. What exactly causes the spokes is unknown, but their re-emergence, combined with a Hubble planetary observing program, will provide opportunities to study them in greater detail. Scientists hope to get to the bottom of not just what the spokes are but why they only emerge seasonally, disappearing and reappearing at certain times in Saturn's year. We first discovered Saturn's spokes in images from the two Voyager probes, which flew past Saturn in 1980 and 1981, respectively: temporary streaks and smudges that usually appear as radial features, moving with the rings as they orbit Saturn. Further observation and analysis revealed more oddities. The spokes usually appear dark from above, while from below, they typically appear bright, and they're not always there. Typically, the spokes appear only in Saturn's spring and autumn, for the eight-year period centered around the equinox, and disappear during summer and winter, for the period centered around the solstice.

4.Scientists Have Found an Invisible Mysterious Galaxy

Using Gravitational lensing, scientists discovered an extremely distant and dark galaxy that's been impossible to see until now. It's been named FAST J0139+4328, and it's not emitting any optical light. In fact, it's barely emitting any light at all.

Using the ALMA telescope in Chile and Einstein's theory of relativity, scientists observed a young galaxy in the early universe that is invisible in nearly every wavelength. The young, star-forming galaxy is filled with dust and gas, and formed 2 billion years after the Big Bang

— an era more than 11 billion years ago, when the universe was about one-sixth its current size. Dim, distant and choked with dust, the object is nearly invisible in every wavelength of light. However, a trick of gravity initially predicted by Albert Einstein has given researchers a rare look at the "invisible" galaxy. "Very distant galaxies are real mines of information about the past and future evolution of our universe," lead author Marika Giulietti, an astrophysicist at the International School of Advanced Studies in Italy, said in a statement. "However, studying them is very challenging. They are very compact and therefore difficult to observe. Also, because of distance, we receive very weak light from them." The team took advantage of Einstein's theory of general relativity to observe the distant galaxy. The theory says that massive objects — like galaxies or, sometimes, individual stars — distort the space around them, so any light passing by gets magnified. This means that researchers can use massive objects as a cosmic magnifying glass to view other, more distant objects, but only when they line up just right. The effect, known as gravitational lensing, has helped astronomers view some of the earliest galaxies in the universe.

5. What is the SUPERNOVA

On average, a supernova occurs once every 50 years in a galaxy the size of our Milky Way. Put another way, a star explodes every second or so somewhere in the Universe and some of those aren't too far from Earth.

A supernova is the biggest explosion that humans have ever seen. Each blast is the extremely bright, super-powerful explosion of a star. These spectacular events can be so bright that they outshine their entire galaxies for a few days or even months. They can be seen across the universe. About 10 million years ago, a cluster of supernovae created the "Local Bubble," a 300-light-year long, peanut-shaped bubble of gas in the interstellar medium that surrounds the solar system.

6.Moon Dust Could 'Shield' Earth from Global Warming

When you get too warm at the beach, you simply sit beneath your umbrella, using it as a shield from the sun. Now Scientists suggest Earth should do the same thing-lunar dust particles can be used as a shield to block 1 to 2% of the sun's radiation

A new paper, published in PLOS Climate, explores the potential of using moon dust to block just enough of the sun's radiation to mitigate the effects of global warming. According to the team, a sunshield's overall effectiveness would depend on its ability to sustain an orbit that casts a shadow on Earth. "If we took a small amount of material and put it on a special orbit between the Earth and the sun and broke it up, we could block out a lot of sunlight with a little amount of mass," said lead author Ben Bromley, professor of physics and astronomy at the University of Utah. The paper tested different properties of dust particles, quantities of dust and orbits that would be best suited for shading Earth. "Because we know the positions and masses of the major celestial bodies in our solar system, we can simply use the laws of gravity to track the position of a simulated sunshield over time for several different orbits," said study co-author Sameer Khan, Utah undergraduate student. According to the study, two scenarios were particularly promising—at least in computer simulations. In the first scenario, the authors positioned a space station platform at the L1 Lagrange point, the closest point between Earth and the sun where the gravitational forces are balanced. In simulations, the researchers then shot particles from the platform to the L1 orbit, and tracked where the particles scattered. When launched precisely, the dust followed a path between Earth and the sun, effectively creating shade. In the second scenario, the researchers shot lunar dust from a platform on the surface of the moon toward the sun. They found that the inherent properties of lunar dust were just right to effectively work as a sunshield. The simulations tested how lunar dust scattered along various courses until they found excellent trajectories aimed toward L1 that served as an effective sunshield.

7.Superfood For MARS

Spirulina is multicellular blue-green algae and a Superfood. It is used as a dietary supplement. Scientists have created a computer controlled photobioreactor to demonstrate how this can be grown on Mars. Spirulina is now considered to be an ideal crop for Martian colonies.

Researchers have explored the possibility of spirulina, a high protein 'superfood', becoming an effective food source for sustaining long-term life on the red planet.

Because water is a rare commodity on Mars, future colonies will need nutritionally dense food that doesn't require much water to thrive. Spirulina is a cyanobacteria with those qualities. Scientists decided to see if they could mimic Martian regolith conditions to grow spirulina by hydrating it with urine. That's right, urine. By varying elements of Martian soil and urine to gauge any differences in results, the team was able to determine the optimal growth pattern. The results showed that spirulina is, in fact, a great candidate for a food source for Martian colonists.

8. What are the Gravitons

There are 17 known elementary particles: 6 leptons, 6 quarks, but only 5 bosons. There's one force carrier missing – the graviton. The Standard Model predicts that gravity should have a force- carrying boson, as graviton. Gravitational waves are, theoretically, formed from gravitons

According to the Standard Model, there are 3 families of elementary particles. When we say 'elementary', scientists mean particles that cannot be broken down into even smaller particles.

The three families are leptons, quarks, and bosons. Leptons and quarks are known as Fermions because they have a half-integer spin. Bosons, on the other hand, have a whole-integer spin. What does this mean? Spin, in the context of quantum physics, refers to spin angular momentum which is a quantum property intrinsic to each particle, even if that particle is stationary. Leptons include electrons, muons, tau particles, and their associated neutrinos. Quarks are tiny particles that, when joined together, form composite particles such as protons and neutrons. Particles formed of odd numbers of quarks, usually three, are called baryons, and those made of two quarks are called mesons. Bosons are force carriers — they transfer the electromagnetic force (photons), the weak force (Z and W bosons), the strong nuclear force (gluons), and the Higgs force (Higgs boson). Detecting graviton will be no easy feat. Gravity is the weakest of the four fundamental forces. You might not think so, after all, it keeps your feet on the ground, but when you consider that it takes the entire mass of the planet to generate enough gravity to keep your feet on the ground, you might get a sense that gravity isn't as strong as, say, magnetism can be, which can pick up a paperclip against the gravitational pull of Earth. Consequently, individual gravitons do not interact with matter that easily — they are said to have a low cross-section of interaction. For now, gravitons are purely hypothetical. Ref source: CERN; Space.Com; Keith Cooper

9.Researchers Created Self- Growing Bricks for Mars

Scientists have used bacteria & fungi to heal cracks in concrete. These self-growing bricks could one day build habitats and other structures for human explorers on the red planet. The concept involves bacteria & fungal spores, and a bioreactor on mars.

The concept would involve sending bacterial and fungal spores and a bioreactor to Mars. The bioreactor is needed for the microbes to survive because Mars' natural environment would be too harsh for them. But Mars would provide the rest of the necessary ingredients for the self-growing bricks, including dust and soil, sunlight, nitrogen, carbon dioxide, and water from melted ice. In turn, the bacteria can produce oxygen and organic carbon to support the fungi. The process, once all of these ingredients are inside the bioreactor, would also create calcium carbonate to serve as the glue. The bacteria, fungi, and minerals will bind Martian soil together to form blocks, which can later be used to make floors, walls, and even furniture.
The team is building a bioreactor to calibrate the atmosphere, pressure, temperature, and illumination

required to grow the bricks. The important feature of this technology is its autonomous nature, and it doesn't require any human intervention. It initially just needs small quantities of spores to start this process, and the rest is automatic. Ref Source: NASA

www.ingramcontent.com/pod-product-compliance
Lightning Source LLC
Chambersburg PA
CBHW021402150726

47989CB00005B/2370